A Free Rein

A Free Rein

VIRGINIA LENG
with
Stuart Sykes

Background material by Devina Cannon
Additional Material by Roger Chown

Photography Kit Houghton

First Formula Publishing

PUBLISHER'S NOTE

When I first made an approach to Ginny Leng to 'examine a year in her life' I anticipated a simple series of written pictures — each posed but examined in great detail. When Devina Cannon and later Stuart Sykes assembled the material, in a period which by any sporting life would be considered eventful, I realised that the book could not be the biographical equestrian portrait gallery I had envisaged; this was no still life.

The words in this book owe a lot to a few:
To Heather Holgate and Dot Willis whose patience, good humour and friendship was so critical;
To Val Gates whose responsive professionalism was so valuable;
To Judy Stott whose counsel and sense of purpose was so important;
To Ginny herself, whose open and unconceited manner made the task so refreshing.

The photography was the work of Kit Houghton, at all times a delight to work with.

To all of them, and especially Stuart Sykes, whose writing and editorial skills brought the project together, I owe a debt.

Roger Chown, April 1989.

PS. Thank you Peter Hogan for the use of your picture.

Published by First Formula Publishing, an imprint of First Frost Ltd
in association with
Citibank Savings ➕

First published 1989
© Stuart Sykes and Roger Chown.
ISBN 1 870066 11 1 (P/B)
1 870066 12 x (H/B)

Designed by Lick 'n Stick.
Typeset, printed and produced by Clifford Frost Ltd of Wimbledon.
Colour reproduction by System Colour Ltd.

ACKNOWLEDGEMENTS

It is with grateful thanks to the following people that I was involved in the ultimate competition for any athlete — the Olympic Games.

My mother Mrs Heather Holgate whose tireless energy and enthusiasm seems to get us through the bad patches, Dot Willis my nanny, mentor and great friend, my horses of the past and present, my trainer Pat Manning, the helpful show-jumping tuition from Pat Burgess and Nick Skelton, and the hard working girls in the yard at home, in particular Elaine Pickworth who flew to Korea with the horses and kept us all sane — and those that stayed behind, Anna Telford, Sally Kingdom and Caro.

Organising a trip to Korea for people and horses takes money and hard work — Director General of the BEF Malcolm Wallace has been a friend for a long time and did a tremendous amount to achieve the British Equestrian entries in Korea. Rosemary Barlow, our major fund-raiser, worked every hour to accumulate the huge sum of money needed to send our teams, HRH the Princess Royal — our newly appointed President of the FEI whose support of equestrian participation is invaluable and very evident in Korea as was our team vet and horse physio husband/wife couple Peter and Anne Scott Dunn.

Lord Patrick Beresford, our chef d'équipe, and Henrietta Knight, our Chairman of the Horse Trial selection committee, did everything they could in order to give us the best chance together with the Duke and Duchess of Beaufort's kindness in allowing our team to use their beautiful park at Badminton for training.

Last but far from least, my loyal sponsors, Citibank Savings. Paul Cohen and his wife Pauline are like second parents to me. Their support, along with the energy and enthusiasm of Val Gates has given me the chance of competing in a sport that I love dearly.

Lastly, my sincere thanks go to Mr Sweetnam who, after nine months of niggling pain, operated on my ankle making me 'sound' once more, and able to ride this year.

I do hope you enjoy reading this book, and sharing a year in my life, a special thank-you to Devina Cannon, Stuart Sykes and Roger Chown for making it all possible, it's full of rainclouds but a rainbow appears in the end!

CONTENTS

OBSERVATIONS

PROLOGUE

On Tuesday, 3rd January 1989, World and European three-day event champion Virginia Leng sat up in bed in the London Hospital and asked for a cup of tea. This modest request was quickly followed by an order for scrambled eggs. The size of the pile Ginny got through was not the only thing that took the nursing staff by surprise: at that stage she was not supposed to have come round from the anaesthetic . . .

The last place Ginny Leng wished to be was in hospital. She ought to have been at home in Avon with her mother, Heather Holgate, and their remarkable assistant Dot Willis, supervising the busy schedule prior to Badminton, the first major event of the season. Ginny's teaching trip to America after the Seoul Olympics had done it; while she was conducting her own clinics, the persistent problem with the leg injured in a fall at Badminton the year before was at last properly diagnosed.

Ginny's leg was fractured. Not just badly sprained and severely bruised, but fractured above the ankle — and fragments of bone were now adding to her distress. Had this been discovered at the time of the fall, she would not have made it to the 1988 Olympic Games. She would not have become the only double medal winner in three-day eventing at two consecutive Games. She would have been out of the saddle for three months, and the history books would look very different.

On the eve of Badminton '89, the pain of that leg injury was almost a memory. Virginia had been on a restorative cruise with friends, the tensions of a long and arduous year — on both the public and private fronts — had dropped away, and the spirit that has taken her to the heights of her sport was once more asserting itself. Badminton, it has been said, would not be the same without her. This book traces a year in the life of an extraordinary horsewoman, and the obstacles she and her horses had to surmount between Badminton 1988 and the same event a mere twelve months later.

*And I thought the **horse** carried the saddle . . .*

A WOMAN AND A WAY OF LIFE

When is a three-day event not a three-day event? When it lasts four days. But when is a one-day event not a one-day event? Every time it happens, because it takes three days to happen anyway. Confusing, isn't it; so it may be useful, before examining one very crowded year in Virginia Leng's life, to look at the basic shape of the equestrian year in general. In eventing, as in any sphere, the successful competitor needs a solid foundation from which to launch the winning effort. For Ginny, that foundation comes from Ivyleaze, her mother's home in Avon, and from the people who surround her there: Heather Holgate herself, Dot Willis and the team of girls who help run the stables.

Looking further back, there are grounds for seeing Virginia Leng as an exception to the usual rules governing the rise of an equestrian star. Her first riding lessons came at the age of three, which in the opinion of Heather Holgate was rather late. Born in Malta, where her father was serving with the Marines, she was in Singapore at the age of six, spent the period from her seventh to twelfth years in England, during which she had the disconcerting experience of seeing the family house burn down, then went off to the Philippines. Her most notable contribution to the life of the convent school she attended would seem to have been the kicking of a football through the Mother Superior's window . . . Returning to England as her father began to suffer from multiple sclerosis,

Virginia Holgate graced Bedgebury School in Kent for a few years, emerging with four 'O'-levels, a five-year-old pony called Dubonnet ('two novices learning together,' she would say), and little or no idea of what she wanted to do. Enter the horses: having groomed at the three-day event in Boekolo, Netherlands, Ginny went on to join the Silverton Pony Club Team, starting inauspiciously in competition by having the whole team eliminated when she failed to wait for the starting bell in her show-jumping round.

Life goes on, however, and by the age of 17 Miss Holgate was a member of the British team which won gold at the Junior European Championships in France. Not only that, but she carried off the individual honours as well. She contrived to complete the Badminton course on her first appearance there in 1974, won on Jason at the mini-Olympics in Montreal in 1975, and seemed upwardly mobile at a rapid gallop. Then disaster struck.

It took the shape of a fall at the Ermington One-Day Event in Devon which left her left arm broken in twenty-three places, needing a four-hour operation to pin and screw bones — while the majority of the specialists consulted advised amputation. Five months out of the saddle did not blunt the Holgate ambition, however, and by spring 1978 a maturing competitor came into partnership with two maturing horses. Night Cap and Priceless ·were their names, the latter proving particularly appropriate.

11

There is no need to enumerate here all the ups and downs — literally — of Virginia Leng's career. Suffice it to say that in 1982 she was a member, on Priceless, of the gold medal-winning British team at the World Championships in Luhmuhlen; took team silver for Britain at the European Championships a year later on Night Cap, and won Burghley on Priceless; took both horses to the Los Angeles Olympics in 1984, taking team silver and individual bronze; enjoyed a remarkable Badminton in 1985, finishing first on Priceless and third on Night Cap, and won the first of her European Championships on Priceless at Burghley in the same season, with a team gold for good measure. On to Australia, 1986: Virginia became World Champion, thanks again to Priceless, and finished the year with the MBE for services to riding.

National champion for the third time running in 1987, she also took second place in a Stockholm competition on Master Craftsman, then a seven-year-old. 'It was the first time we got the feeling he might make a genuine international horse,' she recalls. 'He was, we also believed, the only chance we had of getting a horse to the Olympic Games in 1988. But I had never been a great fan of his. He didn't suit me at all; he was too big and gangly, and I found him altogether uninspiring. Stockholm that year was the final test for Crafty: if he didn't go well I had decided to sell. But I confess he impressed me a great deal, so the decision was made to keep the horse and try for Seoul. You can't just buy horses the way you do cars, you see. There is a four- or even five-year plan that goes into their preparation for major competition, and at that stage we simply had no chance of another coming along. It was a very risky position to find ourselves in, because you never know what may befall the animal — to say nothing of the rider!' A second European Championship success followed in the autumn of 1987, on Night Cap this time, and like his stablemate and great contemporary Priceless he was then

Team at work —
Heather, Ginny and Dot.

retired — each as a champion, sound enough to enjoy years of galloping cross-country.

Much of the credit for this catalogue of successes must go, as Ginny is the first to acknowledge to two other people: Heather Holgate and Dot Willis, and in an Olympic year their roles were again to be crucial. 'None of us would do this if we didn't enjoy it,' says Ginny, 'and we've continued to do it over the years *because* we've enjoyed it and it seems to work as a system. I don't think Mummy or Dot would do it unless they genuinely wanted to — there's no martyr syndrome here.'

Heather, a most experienced and accomplished rider in her own right, takes great responsibility for the schooling of younger horses and many of the routines where the older animals are concerned, while also helping her daughter organise the financial side of a complex international operation. Dot Willis, who moved to Ivyleaze in 1981 as Ginny's full-time trainer, was before that a freelance travelling instructor and still teaches, 'mostly local regulars at novice and intermediate level who are keen, and who put up with the fact that they can't always come when they want to, knowing that if I can fit them in I will. I came when Ginny was in her first year on the senior team, and I used to teach her practically every day. Now the situation has evolved and changed somewhat, and we form more of a working partnership.' Dot, incidentally, will not trust anyone else in the yard to handle all the tack!

Everyday routine at Ivyleaze sees the trio trying to have breakfast together two or three times a week, depending on whether Ginny has gone to canter early, or Heather is out hacking. 'A telephone free-for-all,' is how Dot describes the rest of the morning, while on the horses' work front they will hack at 0830, or earlier if it is a cantering day — often at 0600 between February and April. On an event day, Dot is driver to Ginny and herself — clearly having acquired a taste for the new Porsche — while Heather heroically takes horses and lorry. 'The rider has to be given as good a chance as possible,' explains Dot — a slow driver by her own admission. 'I sometimes think the other riders wonder if Ginny would be quite so good if she weren't supported in this way, but she has the sense to let herself be helped. The professionalism of the attitude has changed so much in the last ten years, and with it the demands we make on the riders.'

Completing the Ivyleaze team are the four girl grooms, all recruited by advertisement (the most recent attracted 68 replies) and dedicated to the care of the animals. They take their three-week holiday between November and January, otherwise settling for a long weekend every six weeks, and bringing to their work the enthusiasm and energy of the 17- to 19-year-old youngsters they are. For Virginia herself, a day spent up in London for meetings is looked foward to as a day off the working routine, even if it does mean an even earlier start to exercise three horses before climbing into the Porsche.

Where the training of the horses is concerned, the occasional kiss has a lot to do with this team's success. Not in the way one might think, mind you — have *you* ever tried kissing a 16-hand hunk of horseflesh, however well the two of you get along? 'One of our sayings,' smiles Ginny, 'is "KISS — Keep it simple, stupid". Sometimes we start getting a bit high-powered and technical, at which point one of us will turn around and say "Kiss", which brings us down to earth again. This little in-house phrase came from my father: it was written on his school report at an exam once, and he said, "Excuse me, Sir, what do you mean?".'

On the personal fitness front, Virginia Leng does some running to keep in shape, building up steadily — and fighting the urge to indulge a taste for chocolate. 'Perhaps this comes from my days as an anorexic schoolgirl, but I *am* a hoarder: I tend to have the odd Lion bar stashed

Clothes horse for the day — the Citibank lorry.

away, which I will never eat. They're just there in case — I basically don't eat chocolate biscuits, but you do find them in the most unusual places. For example, there's one in my hat-box right now . . . Always some available, hidden in the car, the desk, the lorry, and people tend to open glove boxes and find a three-year-old chocolate bar. At a three-day event, for the only time in the year, I feel I have the excuse to eat them — it's quite extraordinary!'

There are other, more obvious forms of therapy. 'If I'm getting really tired, getting towards a big event, I love to tape an old movie, something really pathetic like *Casablanca,* and that does me the world of good. For me, that's truly decadent: a good steak and a really good old movie, once in a while. It's not so much the meat and the movie I'm enjoying, it's the decadence itself, I suppose. But my favourite food of all, at a three-day event — which is the only time I ever eat it — is fried egg sandwiches . . .'

Getting back to the serious side of the business, Dot Willis has her own clear-sighted ideas as to why Virginia Leng is where she is in the equestrian world, and it does not all depend on the Ivyleaze team. 'Determination and dedication; willingness to accept education, further education and specialist education — when it is there, to pick it up, think about it and deal with it. She is now a complete rider, because she is very much aware of the relationship between flat work and jumping. Event people tend to think of them as separate, because they come in three separate phases. Ginny understands the thread between them — some others do as well, in a different way, but there are a tremendous number who neither think about it nor accept it.' Those phases of the three-day event, and indeed the whole structure of this peculiar combination of equine and human talent, are mysteries which must now be made clear.

*   *   *   *

'Who in their right mind would get up at

14

The incomparable Priceless in conversation with his rider.

five in the morning, put their wellington boots on because it's lashing down with rain, pack their picnic basket and sit by a fence all day?' Virginia Leng asks the question, and she better than most knows the answer: the army of volunteers who create the stage on which she will parade her talents. 'You've got the dressage judges, the collecting ring stewards, very often the course builders; you've got the fence judges for the different classes, first aid people, commentators who themselves very often aren't paid, secretaries certainly aren't paid — you've got a complete volunteer service, and it's pretty extraordinary in that respect. And the enthusiasm of some of these people is fantastic: there's a chap that does the show jumping collecting ring at Brigstock — he is so charming, and he absolutely adores it. His whole year revolves around that day. He gets to meet Mark Todd, gets his autograph, chats away; he's maybe 48 or 50, and he's there every year — and just one of the people who give up so much of their time.

'I feel quite strongly about these people, because basically we never thank them. I try to go and thank the secretary and the people in the scoring bus, and we always send a postcard to the organisers of the competition after we've been, but nobody ever gets the chance or shall we say even bothers to go and thank the fence judges, or the first aid people. And they're doing it for us, let's face it, they're not doing it for anybody else. So who thanks them?'

What of the structure of this sport itself? Ginny Leng admits it may be more complex than the average television spectator has been able to grasp. Such people would not know you have to do so much mileage on roads and tracks at so many yards a minute before you get to steeplechase, before you go cross-country. 'I certainly didn't know,' she admits, 'when I first went to Badminton to watch. I thought you warmed up and went cross-country. Perhaps we should take it by stages, and try to help people understand what we are trying to achieve?'

The three-day event is designed to test all-round horsemanship, and the partnership of horse and rider under a variety of conditions. The first day embraces the dressage test; day two takes in the speed and endurance test; the third and final phase comes on day three with the show-jumping. It all sounds straightforward enough, but life is never as simple as it seems.

A charitable view of a model career.

Dressage is a means to an end as well as an end in itself. To the uninitiated, this series of apparently mechanical manoeuvres in which a horse does apparently unnatural things with its feet and legs is a contradiction in terms; to the rider, it is a form of discipline without which the other aspects of a three-day event could not be tackled. 'Even if we didn't have a dressage *test*,' insists Virginia, 'we would still do dressage work anyway. It wouldn't re-

16

One of the peaks: Virginia Leng, European Champion 1987.

move the need to do dressage training at home, because without that the horse would not learn the discipline required to get him over steeplechase fences, or to complete a show-jumping round. It is, in a sense, the very foundation of what we are trying to achieve.

'If you watch the show jumpers, they all do dressage too. It's a slightly different form of dressage, perhaps, technically, but basically they have to do the dressage to get their horses jumping properly.' The idea of dressage (from the French verb *dresser*, to train or teach) is military in origin, and indeed the Germans still use that term to describe this phase of eventing. 'The original idea,' Ginny recalls, 'was that the horse would stand still in a parade, or on the battlefield: the horse was being trained almost like a gun-dog. On the steeplechase side, the horse would gallop across the countryside, jump fences, let his rider get off and engage in combat, then carry on unconcerned.

'What is fascinating is that if you watch a horse loose in a field he actually does dressage of his own accord. Grand Prix dressage, as in *piaffé* or *passage*, too: if a horse is really excited — he's seen the hounds, or something like that — he will start doing passage and flying changes naturally in the middle of a field, and he'll do extended trot, which is wonderful to see. He's never been trained to do those movements, he just does them. It's when the rider starts telling him he wants him to do them *now* that you start getting involved with the character of the horse! Mental attitude, physical ability, power: they can all basically do it, but the rider has to graft discipline on to what is that basic instinct in the animal.'

The point is summed up in one of Virginia's favourite quotes about her sport, one which came, fittingly enough, from a now-forgotten German source: 'The horse already knows how to be a horse; the art of *horsemanship* lies solely with the rider.' 'It's so true,' she adds. 'They already know how to do everything, it's just a question of whether the idiot on top can channel it or not.'

Thus the most important element in the making of a championship horse is its temperament, as, many will contend, is the case with athletes in any discipline. An abundance of talent may be betrayed by temperament, the inability to cope with what we now all too often call pressure. 'It is exactly the same with a horse,' says Ginny. 'You can have an animal with huge talent, but if its temperament is not right you might as well not start.' Murphy Himself, as later events would show all too clearly, was the perfect case in point. 'Murphy is a brilliant horse, but he has a very difficult temperament. He is the strongest horse I have ever tackled, and what is interesting is that his temperament was clear when you compared his reaction to my Badminton fall with that of Lucinda Green's horse when she too came a cropper. Lucinda's horse never moved: he stood there, waiting for her to get up and walk over to him to remount. What did Murphy do? He got the hell out of there, and if I'd had my foot stuck in the stirrup there is no way that horse was going to stop — I would have been dead. The reason Priceless was so brilliant was that, while he didn't have the natural talent of a Murphy, his temperament was exceptional. Night Cap was very genuine, but he tended to be a little neurotic. Horses are very like people, you know: all that little bit different. Crafty was something else again — very laid back, easy come, easy go.

'To illustrate what I'm getting at, I can recall one of the most emotional moments I have ever experienced. It was with Night Cap at the European Championships in Luhmuhlen. His problem was always dressage: he was quite brilliant at the discipline itself, but he couldn't cope with noise. If he heard clapping, he'd break out in a muck sweat, become very tense and start shaking. At a major championship, you have to be in the warm-up arena just outside the main grandstand area as a rule, and of course there's going to be clapping when the horse in front of you has finished his test. So there was no way I could have the horse two miles away and time it so that I cantered up and got into the arena and missed the clapping.

'So I tried all manner of things: a brass band playing in his stable . . . rent-a-crowd from the village to clap while he did dressage here . . . I took him to a show for four days running just to hear all the noises: we went to a great deal of trouble to accustom him to all the noises he would encounter, and it just wasn't working. In Luhmuhlen, though, something happened to that horse. It must have been the sense of occasion, but the horse heard the clapping and went berserk. I thought, "That's it, we've stuffed it." So into the grandstand area we went, and trotted round the outside of the arena, and he was like a piece of concrete. Of course he wasn't going to get any good marks in that attitude; but then the bell went, and whether it was me suddenly relaxing or what, I heard the horse take a huge deep breath, and he went as supple and soft and relaxed as he always was at home, and did the best dressage test he's ever done. It was just extraordinary, and I knew if he could do one of his brilliant tests we had a damned good chance. But it was so totally unlike him to do that, it was a very strange moment, and one which I shall always remember.'

So much for dressage and its purpose and effects. One of the best ways to understand Day Two, which brings the speed and endurance test, is to use the analogy with rallying: making allowances for the difference between horsepower as represented in a mechanical object like a car and horseflesh as expressed in the handsome shape of a Master Craftsman, the idea is the same — to cope with a number of tests and types of terrain within an optimum time and while incurring as few penalties as possible.

The day takes shape in four phases. Phase A, Roads and Tracks, incorporates some 5,280 metres approximately, to be covered at 220 metres per minute; Phase B is steeplechase, taking in ten brush fences to be jumped at racing speed, i.e., 2,700 metres at approximately 690 metres a minute; Phase C returns to Roads and Tracks, normally approximately 8,000 metres again at 220 metres a minute. Then comes a horse examination and the ten-minute halt box — rather like a service halt on a rally, where the public can enjoy a close-up view of horses and riders between stages.

Phase D is the cross-country: approximately 6,000 metres to be taken at 570 metres a minute. Speed and endurance, that is the essence of the exercise. Roads and tracks are the endurance factor, basically, given the distance covered — about 17 miles at the end of the above. The speed works out at a pretty fast trot, or walking and cantering. The rider is given a time within which to do each phase; going over the time incurs heavy penalties, but going too fast simply means exhausting your horses and thus penalising yourself.

'Steeplechase,' in Virginia Leng's view, 'is one of the most difficult phases. It's like doing the Grand National, but all on your own. You are going fast and you're jumping fences at speed, which is an area where we're not professionals in any sense. We are not trained, as jockeys are, to jump brush fences at speed. We're therefore doing the same job, on our own, without a great deal of practice or experience, so that's why Phase B tends to be a danger area; quite regularly you have falls on the steeplechase. Very rarely do you have a refusal, as the fence is so straightforward that any self-respecting horse is going to jump it. But it's a question of whether the rider and horse are in tune together to jump these fences at a speed they're not used to going at, because it's a great deal faster than the pace at which you take the cross-country element.

Dot Willis — 'Nanny, mentor and great friend'.

'And another thing to bear in mind is that you never do a steeplechase course at a one-day event, so you end up doing it — if you're lucky — twice a year, or at as many three-day events as you go to. That particular phase is always a little bit hairy, because it's the one area you haven't really practised, and speed kills. In fact you try *not* to practise that, because the more you practise the more likely you are to have an injury to the horse.'

Back to Roads and Tracks for Phase C: same time, same speed — trot/slow trot or canter/walk. Then the rider comes into the ten-minute halt box, near the start of the cross-country. At that point the horse is checked by a veterinary surgeon to make sure he is not blowing too hard and is sound to continue. At the same time the rider gets off, obeys the call of nature or satisfies the craving for nicotine, chats to other competitors and gleans as much helpful information from them as possible, while the horse is taken by the helpers (Dot, Mum, the groom) and washed or sponged down depending on the climatic conditions on the day. All his shoes and studs are checked, he is made comfortable and walked round during this obligatory timed period.

The rider is usually told two minutes before setting off on the cross-country phase, though Ginny always asks for a four-minute warning because she doesn't like to panic! After a countdown, the pair are off on the last phase. Times for each phase of the day will have been notified to the rider the day before, and life of course becomes rather complicated if a particular rider has entered more than one mount.

'At Badminton,' explains Ginny, 'they don't start till eleven o'clock because they like to get those huge crowds in, so you're hanging about and hanging about. If you're riding two horses you're more likely to start at 11:15 or 11:30, so you've done your 17 miles, you're feeling like a damned good gin and tonic, and you've got to get ready to go again. I think we had half an hour last year between getting off one horse and on the other, in which time I had to do his bandages, see he was all right, check the tack and change my number. Phases A, B and C are something the spectators rarely see, unless they know the sport and specifically want to look at the steeplechase; Roads and Tracks are like the parts of a rally between the special stages, and the cross-country is like a special stage and really rather exciting. There is a definite analogy: all-round test of car and driver, all-round test of horse and rider.'

Show-jumping, straightforward enough if nerve-jangling at the end of a major championship, completes the picture of a three-day event. But to revert to the question set at the beginning, when is a three-day event not a three-day event, and what exactly is a one-day event. 'To straighten out this confusion,' says Ginny, 'the only difference at a one-day event is that we don't do Phases A, B and C as described above. But because of the sheer number of entries for a particular event, you may find there have to be two full days of dressage before the cross-country day, before the show-jumping day of a 'one-day event'. Which means it really takes four days, as at a place like Gatcombe Park, where they can't possibly fit all the competitors into one dressage day, and because they want all those lovely crowds they spread the whole net as far as they can and the crowds pay their £8.50 to get into the field each day.'

On the other hand, there are plenty of occasions when the riders *do* undertake each of the disciplines within one day, as at the novice events, ninety-nine per cent of which are held on one day. If a rider has two horses entered, all three tests have to be carried out twice within a very short space of time, often starting very early in the day and finishing equally late.

An example of how weird things can be came for Ginny at Doddington, just down the road from her Ivyleaze base. 'I did my dressage test at nine in the morning, and

21

my show-jumping wasn't until 16:30, so I actually came back home and did a major photographic session for a magazine whilst I was competing. It's probably one of the most extraordinary days I've ever spent. Hours of photographs, back to Doddington, had time to have lunch with my sponsors and then still had time to walk the course again and start doing the rest of the job. By way of comparison, at Whitton Castle, an advanced one-day event, I rode three advanced horses through all three phases before three in the afternoon — absolute murder — I just didn't know whether I was coming or going!'

Flexibility, then, is one of the names of this game, and the sharp-eyed reader will have noticed a variation on the theme in what Virginia said about Doddington — she went from the dressage test in the morning to the show-jumping before the cross-country. Who's fooling whom here? 'There's another confusion, I admit,' she laughs. 'At a one-day event, ninety per cent of the time we do the show-jumping ahead of the cross-country. We feel this is slightly more humane to the horse, because it's just a bit rough on him to go cross-country — our 'special stage', remember — and then say "Right mate, now it's time to go show-jumping . . ." All clear?'

In general terms, however, the shape of a working day at an event leaves little room to pause for breath, let alone dash back home for a conveniently-timed photo call. If there is the odd twenty-minute break, the experienced rider will walk the course yet again, or watch the other show-jumpers, always in the search for that extra little piece of information which might just make all the difference come his or her turn. And in the normal course of events, the Leng lorry is a scene of mad activity, with people dashing in and out with questions about a particular fence, information about a faller, requests for a lifesaving cup of coffee, a sponsor asking for inside information about the course —

in short, the lorry is the hub of a ceaseless cycle of activity.

Just as a rally driver or his navigator must carry in his head a picture of the course ahead, the landmarks and pitfalls, so a three-day event rider must have the clearest possible picture of what lies ahead. 'There's an enormous amount to remember at a three-day event,' is the somewhat rueful comment from Ginny. 'It will vary from three-day event to three-day event, but there are a number of turning flags to watch out for on the Roads and Tracks. At Badminton there are six or so, which is no problem, but jumping ahead for a moment to Seoul, there were something like twenty-two. Now, to use an analogy with another sport again, these have the same importance as the gates on a ski slope — you've *got* to go through them all, and if you don't you're eliminated. That would be a very sad way of ending an Olympic Games, and in fact in Seoul a certain member of the British team (not me, for once, but perhaps we'd better not mention any names) was seen trotting the wrong way having got totally lost, but fortunately managed to get back on the right road again. No outside assistance, remember: if you're spotted responding to a group of Union Jack wavers pointing you in the right direction, you're out, so it can be a bit of a nightmare.

'I think this is one aspect of the strain on our nerves that people may not fully appreciate. When you come to a major championship roads and tracks section, the sheer fright of seeing all those turning flags can be immense. Seoul again: all those rice paddies looked identical! Normally you have a group of trees, a village, a main road — something that corresponds to a map and all its usual variety, something you can recognise. But in Seoul we had to invent rhymes to help us. There was a junction simply called 'Junction', where you came to the spot three or four times and had to go a different way each time . . . The complicated roads and tracks in

Seoul worried me more than anything — because it would be the most *stupid* thing to do. After all, if you have a bloody good fall at least you go down like a hero; but if you miss out a flag, you would never forgive yourself or be forgiven. In Los Angeles, at the previous Games, an Australian rider went the wrong way on the steeplechase and was eliminated. Well, he suffered as you have never seen anyone suffer, and that is one of the major pressures — trying to remember everything, and when a situation arises that is out of the ordinary, keeping your concentration and simply coping with it.'

To underline this essential point, Dot Willis goes back to a three-day event at Boekolo in the Netherlands. 'Flat as a pancake, sandy tracks, all the same — and you're in woods.' Ginny herself recalls a further danger. 'One one occasion in Holland I set off on Roads and Tracks, and some flags had actually been removed by members of the public. I don't know how I managed it — and I'm sure I could never do it now — but I remembered where I was going, took the bit between my teeth and chose the right way. But the bloke before me was lost for two and a half hours! Can you imagine training all that time, all those disciplines with the horse, and then you get lost? The committee were wonderful, because they acknowledged that the flags had been removed, and the horse was allowed to compete because of the circumstances.'

One other aspect of three-day eventing that the public does not suspect is the tacit competition between riders and rule-makers whereby the riders attempt to find a short cut on the roads and tracks. 'It's always been an unspoken rule,' acknowledges Ms Leng, 'that if the competitors can find a short cut once the course has been set, that is one of the fun parts of the competition — trying to outwit the course builder himself. One of the best examples was when we went to Poland, and actually did find several short cuts on the roads and

tracks, which was very exciting. Even more exciting, however, was the fact that we found two short cuts on the cross-country, which is almost unheard of. I was first of our team to go, and the first competitor on the course. We had to go down a long track to its end and jump a fence; then we were supposed to turn left, describe a square and come back. But *we* went down the track, jumped the fence then turned back on ourselves, back along the same track to the second-last fence. The faces of the fence judges, and the general public! One minute they saw me go past and jump the fence, and walked across the course, next moment I was coming full tilt back towards them! Really quite fun . . .

'Mind you, there is a danger involved in spotting the short cuts. You have to remember you're part of a team, competing against other countries, so when you're out walking the course and another team — the Italians, say — come along, then you pretend you're picking roses, or looking at the wonderful scenery. Again in Poland, I remember followiing a Russian on the roads and tracks, and normally the competitor in front is about a kilometre ahead. Next thing he knew, I was ahead of him — and he panicked, because he thought his watch was wrong. He came straight past me again at a flat-out gallop, because he had obviously thought, "My God" — or whatever a Russian would say — "she's in front of me, I've got my time wrong, I must go hell-for-leather to the end of Phase C." I tried to tell him not to worry, I'd found a short cut, but he was Russian, so . . . he stayed absolutely horrified.'

One final circumstance to bear in mind is a fall or other incident which forces the competitors behind to stop. When the riders are walking a three-day event course, they are shown a series of marked posts, perhaps in four different areas, called stopping zones. If a rider has fallen and can't be moved, or a horse is stopped for another reason, a radio message will be sent back and from a good distance away

Family sport, family transport.

the next rider will see a red flag being waved. When the rider reaches the appropriate stopping zone, he will stop his watch and wait until the signal comes to set off again. He may go back as far as he likes to build up speed, go past the marker peg and start the watch again. An official will also have gone through the same timing process to clock the rider in, as it were, and back out once the course is clear.

'The danger is,' says Ginny, 'that once the horse has been allowed to walk he will simply switch off. How to keep his attention, and how long will I be here for? Sometimes it can be an advantage, as it was for me in Gawler when I won the World Championship. There was a long, steep hill, and a couple of people were stopped at the top, and that worked in our favour as it gave the horse time to recover before the next big effort. But if it's longer than five minutes the horse can tie up, and you lose your togetherness.' So far, however, Virginia Leng has never been stopped for a significant period in a three-day event: long may it continue.

Ginny is keen to highlight the role of the girl grooms — her equivalent of a crew of mechanics, who never steal the limelight but perform basic tasks without

which her effort would not be possible. Checking reins and leathers, looking after the horses — they are the bread-and-butter workers who are trained to be as sharp at a halt box as mechanics are in a Grand Prix pit lane. If this team is doing its work, the rider is free to concentrate on what he or she needs to be doing; checklists are drawn up under Dot's supervision, so that if Ginny gets on a horse in a hurry she can assume that nosebands and other important factors are on the right settings. This level of preparation is what distinguishes the top-class rider from the average competitor — and even then, Ginny is perhaps in a class of her own where the small print of preparation is concerned. Others at the top are laid-back — one to the extent of not having walked the Badminton show jumping course before winning the event — but Dot is convinced Ginny's attention to detail is invaluable. 'I know Ginny does not altogether agree but there are a lot of riders, even at this level, who would be better if they copied her in this respect. You can't really educate into people what the leading riders with natural talent have, that allows them to get away without that degree of meticulousness. On the other hand, you can get too technical, and I suppose we would have to say that she is bordering on that — there is a very fine line between the casual and the over-technical.'

Team work, then, is all: Ivyleaze is at the base of Virginia Leng's preparation for competition, her approach to her chosen sport, and the excellence she has achieved in that particular world. Nothing highlights the quality of team work better than a major event: some insight into Ginny's belief in the correlation between individual ambition and membership of a team — as has been the case so often in her representative achievements for her country — may be a useful way of introducing the first major event of the year in question: Badminton.

CHAPTER ONE:

SILVER HORSES AND GOLDEN DREAMS

A constant thread in Virginia Leng's conversation about her sport these days is team spirit: the need to foster it, the desire to retain it, and the urge to pass it on to a new generation of riders following in her illustrious footsteps. 'I feel very strongly about trying to prepare the younger generation for team competition, and what team work in the proper sense does actually involve. All year you are competing against one another to get a place in the team. Then suddenly you're jolly good pals and you're part of a team, and you have to give all your trade secrets away!

,'It is terribly important that the people who are lucky enough to be part of that team are totally honest, and that we can trust one another, because if you can't, there's no way you're going to win a medal. That is a very difficult task, to teach someone, prepare them for that huge change. My first-ever senior team competition was in 1981, and Dot calls it "a true christening". Technically speaking, a rider joining the team for the first time would always be put in the number two slot. Number two is your "weak" slot; one is your pathfinder, the experienced rider and horse you don't necessarily expect to be in the lead, but almost certainly going to go clear and report back clearly.

'Number two, as I say, is your weak link. You don't quite know what that one's going to do, but you just hope to God that with the first chap round and information imparted he'll be okay. Number three slot is equivalent to number one, with perhaps a bit more chance of a good time across country; and number four slot is your hopeful individual. If the team is doing jolly well, you tell number four to go for individual glory as well: he or she is the beneficiary of everything that has gone before. If you're number four you're laughing, because you should know everything and you're supposed to be the best of the lot. More than likely you're going to be

The Priceless Silver Horse.

given the order to go for the individual as well, while at number one there's no way you're going to get an individual medal: you're going round to suss the whole thing out for the others, so it's very like a sprint relay team, where number two is always the most anonymous position.'

The Leng — or Holgate, as she then was — career as a team performer began rather unusually, as it happens. 'I was put number one in my first-ever team, which is very unusual; and as it turned out, that day in Denmark at the European Championships in 1981, I was also the first competitor to go in the whole cross-country phase. The course was so horrific that all the chefs d'équipe got together, which they had never done before, and said that unless the fences were lowered they would not allow their teams to go round. It wasn't until Friday afternoon they decided to lower it, so you can imagine what sort of state I was in . . .

'I was riding Priceless, and I managed to finish sixth and best of the British contingent — I shall never forget it, and I have certainly never been more frightened in my whole life. Everything went wrong, too: I set off on Phase A, and it was foggy — I didn't know where I was. We'd walked it and driven it time and again, but in the fog I just hadn't a clue where I was. When we got to the steeplechase it was beginning to lift, which was more than could be said for the hot air balloon I came across, twelve feet off the ground in the middle of the course. Then the starter began talking, logically enough, in Danish, and we didn't know whether he was counting down, telling us to keep walking round, or what. Then we looked up and saw the clock ticking, and realised the man had given the order to go, so I started fifteen seconds late — and to make that up on a two-and-a-half mile steeplechase course is going some.

'Then I lost my shoe on Phase C, something that very often happens at speed. Then you worry whether the horse is going to get a bruised foot, so I was worried sick all the way round, but fortunately the ground was very good and he was fine. But the whole thing was an absolute nightmare. The point is this: I'm convinced that one of the reasons why the team has done so well in the time I've been a member, which is the last eight years, is

Karen Straker Got Smart in 1988.

26

because we've had excellent team spirit. I was taught, if that is the right way of putting it, by Lucinda Green, and I am trying to teach people like Karen Straker, as is Ian Stark. When we hang our boots up, it's basically up to Karen, and I'm sure that why Britain has been at the top for so long — because of this remarkable "give" between the riders when it comes to a team championship.'

Ginny finds analogies for her experience in all manner of other sports, and the one that comes to mind here is tennis. What would Shriver ever have done, for example, without her doubles partnership with Navratilova? And David Lloyd was a perfect British illustration of the point she is making: not the greatest tennis player in the world by a long string of computer placings, but when it came to Davis Cup and representing his country, particularly with brother John on the same side of the net, the man — and his team — were transformed.

Interestingly enough, however, the team spirit stops short of the extra dimension — the horses themselves. Ginny Leng could not cope, she feels, with having other riders on her horses, or with having to get on their horses in the heat of battle. 'That used to be the case,' she recalls, 'but I'm glad it no longer is. I think the responsibility of lending your horse to someone and then riding it yourself is too great. Mind you, at Badminton in the show-jumping training before we left to Seoul, we'd all sit and watch one another, and the trainer would comment, and then we would all chip in with our own opinions. Karen Straker, for example, hadn't been in that position before. She'd been a member of the Young Rider teams, but at this level the most important thing in our minds was to keep her confidence up: everything we said to her was in a very positive manner. If she had fences down, we'd joke about it to get it out of the way, then come in with the genuine technical side to try to help her find the way forward. Always with a new-

comer, or someone who hasn't been on a team for a while, it's very much on our minds as the old codgers to try to give positive support.'

There is no team manager, as such, no-one automatically to play the kind of role Ginny has just outlined, but the man around whom the team revolves is the chef d'équipe. His is a four-yearly appointment in which the riders themselves have no say, and the recent experience of being led by first Major Malcolm Wallace then Patrick Beresford has been a major contribution to the team's successes. 'He organises everything, tries to make sure everyone is happy, but to some extent leaves it to the older, more experienced members of the team to do their duty and help among the newcomers, especially if something has gone wrong as it tends to do in the build-up to a major championship.

'In my experience things very easily start to go off course, say two weeks prior to the event, when you're all together and the thing is just around the corner. You start riding nervously, saying to yourself, "Last time I jumped, he went really well — should I jump him again? If he goes badly,

Everything under control . . .

27

Golden sun, silver medals, bronzed bodies — Los Angeles 1984.

what an awful way to go to the event." Indecision sets in: at home, just getting ready for Badminton, say, you'd tell yourself not to be such a wimp — if the horse goes badly, you just have to jump him again. But building up to a major team championship you find it hard to make that sort of decision.' Does the British method consist of selecting people on individual merit, or for the contribution they will make to a *team* effort? There was, after all, some criticism of the selection for Seoul of Captain Mark Phillips: was this fair? Virginia Leng is always forthright in her opinions, and the answer is unequivocal. 'No. I've been on several teams with him now, and he is very aware of what is going on in the team, very supportive — he notices if someone is down or upset, and suggests talking to him or her to try to get to the bottom of it. The team is selected on talent and results; however, if there were someone in the team who was difficult, they would be thrown out on their ear and to hell with how good they were. Misbehave, or act against team spirit, and you're out. The quiet ones in the

past have always been encouraged to bear in mind that they are part of a team, and to try to act accordingly.'

What of the team selection process in this vital Olympic year? Ginny was named on the long list after Badminton, then a final trial took place six weeks before Seoul. She knew she was going to the Olympic Games six weeks before the team left, and was told she was one of three members picked for the actual team before they left. Karen Straker and Lorna Clarke did not know until they got to Seoul whether they were in the team or not. They both knew they were on the same level, and everyone was very honest about it, and knew that the course would be one of the determining factors. The other side of that coin is that Virginia Leng, for all her personal achievements, had been working with Master Craftsman since he was a five-year-old in the confident expectation that at eight he would become an Olympic horse, and she had confirmation of this only six weeks before the momentous event itself . . .

At the start of Olympic year 1988, then,

29

Ginny's situation reflected all of the polarities so far discussed: individual achievement and the desire to be part of a team, personal effort and the dependence on a team, the ambition to do well in a forthcoming major event as an individual and the overriding ambition to be part of the Olympic collective effort. Putting it another way, Virginia Leng was World Champion, European Champion for the second time, and at the peak of her career. A World Team gold medallist, twice a gold medallist in Europe, with Olympic silver and bronze medals in the trophy chest, and an MBE, she was looking forward to enhancing the collection in two particular ways.

The first was by collecting another of the silver horses that reward the achievement of finishing in the top twelve at Badminton, Britain's premier eventing occasion. Beyond that, and at the season's end, was the ultimate goal: Olympic gold, for the British three-day event team and any medal for Virginia Leng herself in the individual event. Los Angeles in 1984 had brought silver and bronze respectively. Did Ginny have the horses, going into 1988, to carry her even higher?

'In general terms,' comes the reply, 'going into a year such as I faced at the start of 1988 you have a very difficult job ahead of you. You've got to get a horse as fit as he can physically be, and yet calm. He's got to be able to run for his life on the cross-country day, but he is also expected to perform a very calm, obedient and *relaxed* dressage test.

'We started the year assuming that Master Craftsman and Murphy Himself would go to Badminton, Murphy would be my Olympic ride and Beneficial was going to have a nice, fun year doing something not nearly as high-powered. Murphy had basically done everything in the book to qualify on paper as an Olympic mount, Crafty had done 75% of what was required, and Ben had done about 25%. All the time, in the back of our minds, there

was this worry about Murphy's control. It was always a major worry.

'I had a pretty good idea I was in trouble at the lead-up one-day events. On paper, they were a great success, because Murphy was placed, he actually won one, and everyone was looking at him as a possible winner of Badminton. But the people at home, including me if I am being honest, were concerned that I didn't have as much control as I needed to have a good run round Badminton. Crafty had done much better in the lead-up to Badminton than I had expected, so my decision to take him there was made very easy. The point is that the lead-up one-day events before Badminton are normally big events: big competition, big fences, they give you a very good idea of how ready your horse is. If you're honest, you'll know very well whether you are set or not. I felt very comfortable with Crafty and reasonably so with Murphy, but there was always this concern at the back of my mind.

'It showed itself in different ways. For example, there was a great deal of bit-changing going on: I was trying out new bits, tighter, looser, to see how I would feel about that mentally. Everyone here was talking about that, involved in it — why does he do it, why does he only do it three-quarters of the way round the course, is it something he experienced as a four-year-old, is it just his mental way? He would only ever do it about five fences from home, which is very difficult to cope with: you had started the course kicking, you ended up out of control.

'At Brockenhurst, the last event before Badminton, he was very strong at the end of the course. I had a Citation bit, which is very severe and has to be treated with a certain amount of respect. It was working very well, but I felt I needed to tighten up the noseband. But there wasn't another event I could practise on, so I had to trust my feeling that with the noseband that bit tighter I'd have that bit more control.

'Beneficial had done quite a few advanced horse trials and he was aiming for Bramham, so that was all under control. But the worst day of the season was when we travelled all the way to Bitkton Horse Trials in Devon, the weekend before Badminton, because I insisted I wanted to do another dressage test and another show-jumping round. The plan was to go there, do those two phases and pull out of the cross-country, because it was too near Badminton.

'So off we went, and it was a long trip, and we also took Beneficial and Ballyhack, who did do all three phases. As luck would have it, the night we were there it absolutely tipped down with rain. All the stables leaked, we were up half the night because all the horses were wet — it was a nightmare. Next day I did two dressage tests which were not too bad and went into the show-jumping and had three fences down *on each horse.* An absolute disaster: they'd been jumping reasonably well, even if they'd had the odd one down unluckily. But there was I, having gone all that way to find that little bit of extra confidence, just give them one more school — a real success! That was on the Sunday, with Badminton on Tuesday . . .'

Bear in mind the other theme that has cropped up continually in Ginny Leng's conversation: pride. The mistake that led to her eliminating her junior pony club team was a desperate blow to that pride; when she first went to an international event, in Holland, as a groom, she was petrified of doing the wrong thing, and almost put off the sport for life. For someone who, until her teens, thought Badminton was a form of tennis, this young lady has developed the keenest sense of what it is that marks top sportspeople, and those in other walks of life, out from the crowd: pride of performance. It took a knock at her first one-day event, when she missed out three cross-country jumps, was eliminated and absolutely mortified. Never allowed by her mother to display publicly her inner turmoil on such

The horse is not the only one needing a breather.

31

occasions, Ginny contained her fury with herself and came up with a personal motto: 'Always forward'. Those words were to come to mind quite often in 1988, when things began to go off the rails, and but for the sense of pride that propels Virginia Leng, and the desire to be a part of a winning team, the rest of the year might have looked very different indeed.

Should anyone doubt that pride and its consequences, Ginny recalls another major team occasion, the European Championships at Frauenfeld, Switzerland in 1983. 'For me it was a disaster. It was the first time I had been asked to go fourth, and I had a refusal. I ended up seventh in the individual event, and the team won a silver medal. If I had known in advance I was going to be seventh, it would have been wonderful. But I'd had that refusal, and I couldn't care less where I had finished. I blamed myself for not winning the gold medal for the team, even though I was the best among three of us who went badly. I felt very disappointed in myself, I felt I had let the team down very badly, because I was last to go — even though the ones who went before me had also had their troubles.' The lady went to Burghley two weeks later, with a horse — Priceless — who had recovered from severe illness, and won her first major title, so the self-belief was restored — no need, after all, to give up her chosen sport. But the way in which a top performer puts pressure on herself, simply by the weight of expectation she places on her own shoulders, is clear, and events at the start of this momentous Olympic year were not doing anything to lift that burden from her.

That pride of performance extends, almost as a matter of course, to the state of readiness of her horses. Here too, the start of 1988 was doing little to help the Leng blood pressure, for she remained unconvinced about Master Craftsman until Stockholm. 'I would never go to a championship, especially a team event, unless I was damned sure my horse was going to put in a good performance. I am simply too

Keeping riders on the right tack.

32

Chef d'équipe: Lord Patrick Beresford.

proud to go somewhere and make a complete mess of it, simply because I wanted to say I had been to the Olympic Games. I'd hate to go, knowing in the back of my mind I wasn't sure the horse could do what was being asked. You're really letting the side down in that case: somebody else would probably deserve to be there a lot more than you did, and do the job a bloody sight better. I don't wish to sound like a martyr, but I couldn't basically go to something knowing the horse wasn't really ready for it.'

Small wonder, then, after the disastrous expedition to Devon on the eve of Badminton, that it was a slightly chastened V. Leng who turned her thoughts to the big event coming up. Still, the basic fitness of the horses was not in doubt, and in all other respects the preparation was perfect. Dot Willis has her own explanation for that confidence-shattering performance. 'It was a combination of many things,' she recalls. 'On paper it's the perfect set-up, doing a competition away from your home environment at the eleventh hour, because the horse doesn't always put in as much effort as you would like it to at home at that stage. But, for many reasons, to do with the weather, the extra distance travelled, tiredness, it became a big effort rather than an easy step.'

Ginny amplifies with her own schedule for that weekend. 'I got up at a quarter to five in the morning, drove the horses to the gallops, galloped them, came back here then got them down to Devon. It was so much simpler to say we wouldn't go . . . Then after all that effort, the driving, the money, the stables, to have three down on each horse. Mind you, when I did it on the second horse I said to myself, "This is a joke," and that was that.' It was, in short, a major excursion that ended in major disaster. If only she had known it at the time, worse was to come for Virginia Leng within the week. Silver horse? Not if one of hers could help it . . .

CHAPTER TWO:

TEAM SPIRIT:
A WORKING SPONSORSHIP

Sponsorship in sport is a subject which seems to provoke one of two reactions; either: 'I really don't understand it' or 'Why do they do it'. The opportunity to attempt to answer both viewpoints has been uniquely provided by Paul Cohen, Managing Director, and Val Gates, Promotions Manager, of Citibank Savings.

In 1987 a contract which Ginny had negotiated with an insurance company, British National Life, came up for renewal. Citicorps had acquired the aforesaid company early in 1986 and in their initial assessment they contemplated the value of the package in past and current terms and in respect of future opportunities. As a company it is not Citibank Savings policy to advertise their services directly to their public. Given this, it was left to Val Gates 'to make something of the deal'. This was something of a challenge to Val — as an Olympic athlete and an ex-professional golfer, she was well aware of the needs of top sports people to have financial support, but banking and horses?!! In '85 when first involved with the Holgate Team there appeared to Val to be opportunities for a sustained and profitable relationship provided the parties defined the 'rules' and understood each other's needs. It was agreed that they would get better PR from transferring the contract to a larger company within the Citicorps group. Therefore Citibank Savings took it over. The 'team' aspect was an important factor — Citibank's sponsorship is for the 'Virginia Leng/Citibank Savings Eventing Team' and it was Ginny who inspired the idea. 'As we all worked so closely together, and as the development of the horses was so much a function of teamwork I felt that a long term deal would be best served if the contract covered *all* our efforts.' This notion had particular appeal to Paul Cohen: 'As one of our principles within Citibank is the ability as a team to handle success and failure equally well, Ginny's request for team support accorded exactly with our own views.'

In looking back, Heather Holgate is as ever direct about the way the original relationship worked and why it continues to work. 'Without the initial contribution we could not have continued in the sport at top level, perhaps not at any level. Tuition is the most important factor in the success of a horse and therefore the most expensive element. This is as true today as it was then.' The income derived from the original arrangement was significant if not huge, and indeed for Heather — although a minor item in the overall cost of the support — 'the transporter was a most valuable contribution.' Today whilst the sponsorship funding is of critical value to the team, the lorry still represents a major factor in the professional presentation of Ginny's eventing, and for Heather, the fact that it does provide a visual demonstration of Citibank's support is as important to her as it is for Paul Cohen, in whose budget the investment is accounted. 'Paul is the perfect business partner — he trusts us and our judgement, he does not seek to control our programme and yet is as committed to us as we are ourselves.' Does this mean that Citibank is undemanding? 'No,' says Heather firmly. 'What he has done with Val is to produce an environment for us which makes us want to support Citibank not just for financial reasons but more because we respect and understand their needs. We do everything possible to assist them. Of course they are demanding but neither Paul nor Val makes demands on us which are unreasonable, and because they don't and because they respect us, we never *feel* pressured.'

In what some may consider to be a blueprint for others Heather made two further points — during the course of another sponsorship proposal made to Heather some while ago, it became obvious that there was a possibility of the sponsors' becoming involved in riding and horse decisions. Even with only the remotest chance of this happening and given that everything else was friendly to the point of affection, Heather still decided against the deal. 'To be successful over a sustained period, decisions made about

A warm relationship.

Events and horses have to be made independently of sponsors' involvement — without that freedom and honesty I believe that sponsors would in the end be less than well served.

My second home!

Backing the right horse.

also one of trust and loyalty and I admire her enormously for making it.'

The right environment is then critical to a sponsorship arrangement and having created it . . . not an easy task . . . it becomes a question of exploiting it to the best for both parties.

When Paul Cohen asked Val Gates to define the relationship, several factors were considered:

— would the deal enhance name awareness for Citibank Savings
— would name awareness increase in the right areas
— could Ginny play a part in product endorsement
— was Ginny's personality employable in a more active way, e.g., increased client hospitality
— were there aspects of PR which could better be employed to assist Citibank's profile
— were there internal activities which could use Ginny's services
— how would the deal be measured in terms of success
— how long should be the long term view.

'By being sponsored as a Team rather than just as a rider, Ginny realised that there would be less pressure on her from within — in a family environment this was not only a gesture of common sense but

Home on the range, with alternative horsepower.

Citibank sales conference.

Very early on, it was decided that product endorsement would be inappropriate — in some ways this was an easy decision as the preciseness of Citibank's products was not easy to associate with a Three Day Event Rider — albeit a champion. The profiles didn't fit.

Name awareness was an immediate target — the lorry was painted, jackets produced, blue and white hoardings and banners bedecked the Event marquees, Citibank Savings name began to be heard with increasing frequency on radio, TV and Event commentaries. Within two years Val Gates concluded that name awareness in the fraternity and within Citibank's target market had increased immeasurably, as had the frequency with which the name appeared in print. Just as relevant though was the realisation that as a direct result of Ginny's active and enthusiastic participation in the client hospitality area, direct contact between Citibank and their clientele — dealers, brokers, and Insurance Companies — had increased substantially and with it customer loyalty.

'It was a gamble to begin with,' says Val Gates, 'but one which looked likely to succeed almost from the very start. On a personal level we gave all we could, and that feeling was reciprocated.' Contractually in 1988 Citibank had Ginny for twelve half days and six full ones. 'Such is the confidence between the parties that even if Ginny had not taken up all her days, Paul Cohen would have been more than happy.'

Internally at the 1988 Citibank Sales Conference, Ginny gave a performance which to quote Val Gates 'had them laughing, had them asking for more and had them enthusing for weeks afterwards.' What had she done? 'Simply been herself — they relate to her because she is not afraid to acknowledge mistakes and because she does not try to be anything other than normal.'

The original questions about sponsorship, particularly the one which asks 'why' are best summed up by Paul Cohen. 'We did it because Ginny and the Team represent perfectly what we try to practise as a company. We did it to increase name awareness in our target market and to enhance client loyalty through a programme of Event hospitality. We did it to improve our PR both externally and within the company. We continue to do it, because it works, and because we have a relationship with the Team which results in their working as hard for us as we do for them. Basically what started off as two teams working together, has become one team . . . and a happy one.'

A careful observer of Virginia Leng would, in 1988, have noticed a number of other business connections — Ebel Watches, Edinburgh Woollen Mills (also major sponsors of Ian Stark) and The Follett Car Group, providers of her Porsche car. These deals were orchestrated by ex-IMG (International Management Group) employee Judy Stott. 'Ginny is a natural — she has a great sense of fun and an ability to relate easily to people from all sorts of environments. Essentially Ginny's deals are endorsements. They are largely a function of trust and mutual reward and the personalities have to fit otherwise there would not be the necessary commitment,' says Judy, a point endorsed by Graham Kimberley of Follett Cars. 'Ginny was approached because she was a winner, because she was in the public eye, and because we felt we could develop a long term relationship with her, in a market which we per-

38

ceived a healthy potential for us.' A simple process? 'No,' says Mr Kimberley, 'we had tried many other forms of endorsement including powerboats and yachting but whilst we enjoyed the experiences, our client base did not respond in the way we had hoped.'

On 31st August 1988, at Gatcombe Ginny was presented with a new Porsche — black this time to replace her silver one. The recipient was as excited as anyone would be to receive such a 'gift'. 'Of course I'm thrilled,' said a beaming Ms Leng. Judy Stott looked pleased too, although much more mindful than her client of the work that would be needed to ensure a repeat performance in 1989. A visitor on the day was Seb Coe, an old friend of Judy's, whose simple remark 'If only people knew just how much had to be done to get to the top,' seemed to encapsulate the whole business of sponsorship and endorsement.

Judy Stott's addition made it clearer. 'Ginny will go to motor shows, meet the press, give sales conference speeches, attend functions, spend long hours in photographic studios, and have to continue winning.'

In 1988 Virginia Leng did all of this. In the other 'horsepower' sport of motor racing, Nigel Mansell, on his change to Ferrari for a reputed three million pounds,

Gatcombe Park 1988 — the new Porsche.

The BEF needs an occasional cheque-up!

Virginia Leng

MASTER CRAFTSMAN

MURPHY HIMSELF

VIRGINIA LENG M.B.E.

World 3-Day Event Champion.
European Champion.
1985, 1987.

NIGHT CAP II

PRICELESS

RANGE ROVER TEAM
CAPTAIN MARK PHILLIPS

made the point that his new deal meant that he would be able to 'concentrate more on his family and his driving,' as a result of his not having to satify so many personal sponsors' needs. Ginny's response? 'I like my sponsors and I accept that I have to work for them and with them. Ours is an amateur sport: we don't get three million pounds for winning but if we don't approach our sport in a professional way we simply won't survive. My sponsors give me the chance to win, and the least I can do is to give them a damn good reason to stay with me.'

The preservation of amateur status relies on the agreement of the British Equestrian Federation to act as a filter for sponsorship payments, a practice which accords with IOC bye laws and FEI regulations. By drawing off 2% of the first £50,000 of sponsor income and 1% of any amount thereafter the BEF is able to put money back into the sport for the benefit of all. Other 'safeguards' concerning the nature, type, and exploitation of sponsorship agreements are carefully laid out in BEF guidelines and for the Ivyleaze team they represent no problems.

'Britain's incredible successes in Eventing would not be possible without a sensible set of rules to cover sponsorship and without sponsors' tremendous support for our efforts' — Heather Holgate. In this context 'Team Spirit' (also the name of a great horse in another discipline) in its widest possible sense, is the foundation of Virgina Leng's Citibank Savings Eventing Team.

Commercial promotion — with BEF approval.

"We hope you enjoy Equorian - it's a great way to support our Olympic team."

(Overleaf) Sponsorship and its consequences: signing on the dotted line with Citibank's Paul Cohen; (inset left) escape: a day out at Henley; (inset right) Badminton '88 — Ian Stark shares his winning moment with Mrs Sam Whitbread — Whitbread sponsored the event — and Mr David Stevenson of Edinburgh Woollen Mills.

CHAPTER THREE:

PRIDE COMES AFTER A FALL

'It takes three months to get fit for one competition like Badminton. What is so sickening is that, if you fluff it, you can't go somewhere else, which is difficult and frustrating. It means that you cannot afford to make a mistake that weekend — unlike, say, Wimbledon, where you simply go on to the next event. In this sport you do not get a second bite at the cherry, and for me this is the most pressurising part of what we do. If you only get halfway round Badminton, you *could* run again three to four weeks later, but you are pushing your luck: it is a risk, and a major physical strain on your horse.'

Virginia Leng's words were said with feeling, and made the more ironic in the light of what did happen to her at Badminton in 1988. Badminton is the greatest test of horse and rider, in a non-Olympic year; and in 1988 the event took on even greater import as a genuine examination of pairings that hoped to perform on the world stage a few months later.

Ginny herself underlines the point. 'This year I shall be going to Badminton with one aim in mind: to try and win Badminton. Last year was quite different: I went there, not to win, but to try to prove I had horses ready for Seoul.' Whichever of those two goals applies, the place — like all the great sporting arenas — has its own peculiar aura, its own feeling.

'What's interesting about Badminton in general terms, as far as the competitor is concerned, is that when you turn up at the horse trials on the Tuesday there is something very weird about the atmosphere. Everybody is very quiet, whereas Burghley, say, is very different: the atmosphere is normally far more relaxed. Badminton certainly has a far more tense atmosphere than any other horse trial I've ever been too. Awe-inspiring, I think, is probably the best way to describe it.

Also, when you first ride at Badminton, it's not so much the fences that strike you, I think, as the sheer sense of occasion. You've never seen so many people, and you have to cope with the fact that there are so many thousands of them meandering around, getting in the way — but you mustn't be rude, because you want to encourage them actually to be there and come again. Some of them don't have the first idea what's going on, the horse has never seen so many crowds in the dressage arena; on the cross-country, before you set off, it's almost as if you don't really want to go out there — a bit like being thrown to the lions in Roman times! You set off down towards the first fence, and there's this whole channel of people waiting to see you — neither you nor the horses have ever seen anything like it. And there are only two reactions: either you rise to the occasion, or you go in the opposite direction.'

Even the greatest can fall foul of this special tension that Badminton engenders, as Ginny is the first to admit. 'I've certainly come a cropper there in my time,' she remembers. 'The first time I had to go first around Badminton, it was a very wet year, and everyone thought it was going to be

THE WHITBREAD CHAMPIONSHIPS
BADMINTON 1988

Hugh Casson 86.

PROGRAMME £1.50

cancelled, we weren't quite sure whether we were going to be asked to go or not. It was slippery, and I really had no inclination to go round at all. I rode a slightly tentative round because of that, and actually paid the penalty because when I got to the water I had a run-out. It was bloody stupid, and I lost the competition as a result. I remember very clearly finishing and thinking what a tentative round I'd ridden, because normally when I ride I'm nervous at the start, but once I jump the first two I'm able to steady down and get on with the job.

'Obviously it's something that affects the inexperienced riders, whereas the likes of Ian Stark and Lucinda Green revel in that atmosphere, and they're the ones who come out on top.' Nor should we think this nervousness afflicts only the human half of each partnership, for it is a feeling that very firmly communicates itself to the horse. 'At that stage, because they are pretty experienced, they realise this is definitely a big event, and what we've really come for. Particularly when you are trying to get them to go well on the flat, for the dressage: once that phase is over, everyone relaxes a little and concentrates on the cross-country.'

And yet, dressage can be the phase that lands a rider in the soup. 'Yes,' muses Ginny, 'although at Badminton it's not necessarily the case: you may not win, after a mediocre dressage score, but you do have the chance to claw back into the competition, your Badminton is not finished yet. On the other hand, the person who leads the dressage doesn't often win the competition as a whole. There's a bit of a superstition among the riders on that point, in fact: no-one really likes to be leading after the dressage, although I have done it in the past at Burghley.'

Further superstition: appear on the front cover of *Horse and Hound* before Badminton at your peril! 'It's happened time and time again,' insists Ginny with only the hint of a laugh, 'and it happened to me. I was on the front cover of *Horse and Hound* on Night Cap and I bloody well fell off at Badminton

'Scottie' and 'Wattie' — what a combination.

45

that week, so nobody wants that particular distinction. We made that known to them about eighteen months ago, as a matter of fact, and they've been quite good about it since. But it happens on the eve of every major competition . . .'

There are ways and means by which the sportsman or sportswoman compensates for the kind of nervous drain Virginia has just described. Reliance on natural talent, which extends, incidentally, to other spheres: Ginny is good at clay pigeon shooting, the hand-and-eye co-ordination that operates in the eventing arena standing her in good stead. She believes most riders are good all-round sportsmen, loves tennis herself and is a competent swimmer and diver.

A more obvious way of facing the daunting ordeal of Badminton, however, is through a form of personal bravery. But when the subject is touched on, Virginia Leng is reluctant to see herself in such a light. 'A lot of people say this to me, you know — how brave we must be. *I'm* not brave, though I know there are people who do qualify for the description — people like Mark Todd, or Scottie (Ian Stark), would have a go at virtually anything, jump out of a plane, have a go down the Cresta Run, whatever. But I'm not like that. I'm very cautious when it comes to doing crazy things. I always deny that I am showing bravery by doing what I do in this sport. The only reason I am able to do it is that I am confident in the horse. If someone asked me to do the Cresta Run, I probably would think hard and then have a crack at it, but other obvious tests of bravery are not for me.'

Confident in the horse? That was not, in all honesty, the case when Ginny approached Badminton in 1988, especially not where Murphy Himself was concerned. Not only that, but neither Murphy nor Master Craftsman had ever competed at Badminton. Murphy had been prepared for the course in 1987, only for rain and

Lucinda and Willy B. — but 1988 was not to be her year.

46

waterlogging to cause cancellation; and then there was that nagging doubt over his temperament and his sheer strength. 'Everyone keeps telling me he is a man's horse,' his rider would say, 'but I am pretty stubborn, and I just hope to be able to bring the best out of him.' On the eve of the 1988 competition, she made a very revealing observation to the outstanding *Daily Mail* sportswriter Ian Wooldridge. 'When I tell you I'm not scared of it,' she confessed, 'you're going to get the wrong idea — I'm actually a wailing wimp. Butterflies in the tummy? I've got damned great cannon balls rolling around my stomach. I'm terribly tense and nervous, because there are two reputations at stake: the horse's and my own. But I'm not scared, in that sense. I have utter confidence that the horse knows what I want it to do. If I get it wrong, then it's my fault.'

Badminton follows a well-trodden path, as far as Virginia Leng is concerned — quite literally. Wednesday is the day for planning Thursday: what time she will be riding, what tack she needs to use, and other details. She has done Badminton so often she knows the Roads and Tracks virtually by heart, but time has to be found to walk the steeplechase course properly. Then the cross-country course takes a minimum of three hours, assessing options should emergencies arise: that second walk round is very time-consuming, and very important. The day is also telescoped because at its end comes a cocktail party, in Badminton House, which demands best bib and tucker from competitors, judges and owners. A lovely occasion, but a lot to prepare for at the wrong end of a hectic day. Ms Leng also makes life harder for herself by having people to dinner at her own flat — on Wednesday, Thursday and Friday of the 1988 event, as it happens.

Having only one horse to ride at Badminton gives the otherwise hard-pressed competitor that little bit of freedom to look at the trade stands, enjoy the

My 'Olympic' horse — Murphy Himself.

47

So far, so good . . .

ancillaries which are part and parcel of any great sporting occasion. The Friday, however, brings the final walk round, always straight round with no stopping: if you come into a corner, you will know by now at which tree you will be stopping, the technical details are clear in the mind: on the seventh white peg, turn, for example. Just make sure you haven't chosen, as your marker, a movable object — that car may not be there next day — or something that the crowds may obscure when you get down to the competition itself.

On the technical front, there is a peculiarity at Badminton which only the initiated could grasp. 'When you come down a particular channel, let's say, the ropes will go straight down, then bulge around the fence. You can never actually take the line you want, because the designer has roped you off. I maintain that fifty per cent of rider errors are because of the ropes, and the fact that he's so clever with them. Normally you can take your own

No water fall.

line, but at Badminton you can't. You have to consider that, plus the fact that things move: the ladies' loo at the end, for example, may have an ambulance parked in front of it next time you come that way. At Badminton, there are just so many more things to worry about, it's a fearsome test of your concentration.'

For twenty-four years Frank Weldon had been Director and Course Designer at Badminton. The 1988 course was to be his last major contribution to the event. Given that the Olympic Games lay ahead, and that Badminton would be the first selection point for the British three-day event team, he had designed a course that was not meant to be unusually severe, but 'with any luck,' as he himself put it, perhaps five per cent more difficult than before. How did the competitors react?

'When we walked the cross-country course,' Ginny reflects, 'the one fence I didn't really like was the Ski Jump, especially the bottom rail, and I wasn't too happy about The Coffin. Those two fences, I felt, had Crafty's name written on them.' Dot Willis didn't share the concern at the time: 'I didn't worry so much about the Ski Jump for Crafty,' she adds, at which point Ms Leng intervenes with some indignation. 'You may not have been, but I was worried about the knees up in the air, thank you very much, for the bottom rail.' 'Funnily enough,' rejoins her trainer, 'that caused me no concern because his hocks would have been underneath him coming down the hill!' A prompt flash-forward to Seoul is made at this point, as discussion grows heated, but that is a story yet to unfold . . . Back to Badminton.

Ginny was also worried about The Coffin for Murphy Himself's sake. The horse had an inclination to do his own thing, and technically The Coffin was a very short distance either side of the ditch. His rider was worried that Murphy would try to bounce it, and get himself into trouble, while Crafty might not be neat enough. 'It was a hell of a size,' she said,

49

'something of a dimension he had never come across before.' 'Coffins,' added Dot, 'are a type of fence you never get to practise over at a one-day event, at least not on that scale.'

Reasonably happy with the course, then? 'As much as one can be,' replies the lady in the hot seat, 'and especially with two horses you'd never ridden round Badminton before. It was a situation I had never found myself in, you normally take at least one experienced horse. Two new horses, and on the same day: it was quite nerve-racking, I suppose!'

Competition got under way on 5th May, Crafty doing a relaxed and competent dressage test, but there was an ominous problem with Murphy Himself. One of the side attractions which appeal so much to the thousands of spectators at Badminton are the Whitbread drays, and their own marvellous horses — marvellous, that is, for everyone except the Badminton competitors. 'They're great fun for everybody, but a pain in the neck for the dressage people,' claims Ginny, 'because they really do frighten the horses. They came right past me as I was in the collecting ring, and I thought, 'Oh my God, any minute now this thing's going to go berserk underneath me.' He got a little bit up-tight as they rattled along past us, then he did his own performance in the arena: at the end of the dressage he did a real *levade*, a back kick, and nearly landed in the judges' laps. People may have seen me give a little smile at that point, but the teeth were clenched and I could have slaughtered him . . . Basically I was disappoined with Murphy and pleased with Crafty at that stage, though a little bit disappointed also with Crafty's actual mark: we thought he deserved a little bit more, but that's the sport.' Crafty ended up fifth, with Murphy 14th after the dressage phase.

On to the steeplechase, where Crafty gave her a very strong ride in his own right, giving rise to concern over control. The horse was just beginning, in a way, to learn what life was all about, and Ginny was surprised at his behaviour — he hadn't been that strong before. A bit change, perhaps? Not the time and place, just get on with the job. Come the cross-country phase, and he was very strong there as well. 'I couldn't quite let him off the hook, so consequently he had six time faults, which was slightly annoying — because somehow I should have been professional enough to have thought about it, or done something about it. But I will know for next time that for a three-day event he is stronger than for a one-day, which is the opposite of how they normally are.' In all other respects, however, Master Craftsman responded beautifully, giving Ginny 'a much more grown-up, classy and mature ride than I could have expected.' The only jarring note was his strength in between fences — a horse that pulls is a horse you go slower on.

'We had only one nasty moment,' she recalls, at the Irish bank. 'He took off a wee bit early and stumbled when he landed, but recovered well.' Over to Dot to explain why: 'The only reason he didn't fall was because *you* weren't out of balance, you kept him up!' Back to the ten-minute halt box, then, to get the other horse ready for his cross-country challenge — and now the atmosphere changed perceptibly. 'Everyone was really weird,' is how it strikes Virginia in retrospect. 'I could sense a sort of dread from Mummy, from Dot, and from everyone who was there with us. None of them, basically, wanted me to ride Murphy, though no-one would say it. But there was a real sense of that in the air, and I thought "Well, damn it, I'm going . . ."'

'You can't stop the way you think,' Dot chimes in, 'but you can stop yourself saying something negative. But Crafty had gone well — in fact she was in front after his cross-country — and she suddenly had her Olympic horse, there was no real need for her to go on Murphy Himself. The feeling, in one sense, was totally ecstatic, and I think we just didn't want her to go

50

Vet check — horse and rider both sound at this stage.

and overdo it.' But the theme of pride is already strong in this narrative, and sure enough the Leng pride surfaced again.

'I just didn't want to be beaten by a horse,' is the matter-of-fact statement. 'I'd never been beaten by a horse before, and I wasn't going to start then. And Murphy Himself, taking nothing away from our other horses, is the most naturally talented jumper I've ever been on. I knew bloody well the horse could do it . . .'

Murphy Himself was outstanding on the steeplechase, never threatening to take over through his own sheer strength, and leaving rider and entourage much happier than they might legitimately have expected. 'We've cracked it,' was the general feeling, and Dot's own description of his performance was 'copybook stuff'. The cross-country began well enough, 'My only criticism,' adds Ginny, 'is that he took a stride out at the big hedge with the big ditch behind it. I asked him to take another stride, as I didn't want him to stand back too far given that there was a big ditch on the other side, but he didn't listen. He just stood off it, and cleared it by miles, and I

thought, "Oops . . ." There are two more hedges later on, the Aintree fences, which normally ride four strides holding, or three really big yahoo strides. I held for four, because I didn't want the horse to open up — once he did, I knew we would be in trouble.

'And the little so-and-so only took three . . . I knew at that point we were all right, but I'd better not let him do that again, otherwise we might be in trouble. He settled, jumped the next twelve or so fences including the water quite beautifully. Then came the Normandy Bank, the one before the dreaded Ski Jump. He jumped the Normandy Bank just like a pony club fence, then I came round the corner to the Ski Jump, throttled right back, and all seemed fine. Then he went to look over, just to pop, which is what I had planned. Then — quite extraordinarily — he changed his mind. If you watch the video, he went just a step, then you see him just change his mind and go splat . . . and off I went, and that was that.'

How matter-of-fact she makes it sound.

51

Dot was worried about Murphy. In hindsight it showed.

It looks easier from this angle.

In reality, she landed with the sort of thump that made her feel every part of her body had been pushed skyward, though the one part that suffered most was her ankle. By a curious coincidence, Commander John Bertram, the surgeon who had played such a significant part in saving her arm eleven years earlier was on the course as one of Ginny's guests. Two fences further on, he heard the news of her fall. 'He arrived at the ambulance tent saying this was the last time he was ever coming to an event, as I always fell off! He took a look, discussed the ankle with the course doctor, and decided it wasn't broken. A nod, a wink, and he told someone to put ice on it. He knew jolly well that I would ride if I felt like it, but it was a weird feeling not to have seen him for ten years and suddenly have him there looking after my ankle.'

The clearest thing in Virginia's mind at that stage was her decision to part company — this time permanently — with Murphy Himself. 'That night, my ankle was enormous — and all sorts of colours, purple, black, green. I couldn't bear anything on it, not even the bed covers, so we fixed up a sort of cardboard box to take the weight off.' That pain apart, the physical

'Murphy and I parted company . . . for ever.'

53

aftermath, how was the Leng psyche responding to this disaster? 'Complete and utter defeat,' is the honest response. 'My pride was so damaged — I've got *such* pride, it's awful to think of it. He'd won Burghley, and various other things. And there was the small additional matter of the Olympic Games. When I saw my ankle, I felt sure it was broken, so in many, many ways, it was defeat all down the line.'

There seemed a glimmer of light in this all-enveloping darkness, when the first aid people told Virginia her ankle was not broken after all — a judgement that did not sit easily with her own feeling. 'You *know* when you've broken something: I just couldn't believe it when they said it wasn't broken. Certainly I don't wish ever to be in the pain I endured on show-jumping day. I could never do it again.' Not that the spectators who watched her, next morning, give a television interview on a borrowed crutch, or go to the 11:30 Badminton church service, would have suspected what she was putting herself through.

With her usual canny eye for what is what, Dot Willis knew exactly what was going through her charge's mind. 'She was spurred on by the total determination of the competitor; by the feeling of defeat at the hands of that horse; the silver horse; and by the thought that she had to qualify the horse for the Olympic Games.' If the last of those considerations was not uppermost in the Leng mind, it certainly was in Dot's.

The spirit of the competitor: first and foremost, Ginny Leng had not yet completed the Badminton course for 1988. For any rider who does, there is already a sense of achievement, to say nothing of the nice plaque and rosette that mark the feat. There is also a bonus for the groom, in the shape of £150 for each horse that does complete, so there is a slight additional pressure there . . . 'I love the fact that this horse trial is generous in that way,' admits Virginia, 'and I also remember being 25th at my first Badminton, despite a run-out

and a very slow cross-country, and I was absolutely cock-a-hoop.'

Just completing the course, therefore, was very much on the lady's mind. Unfortunately, her ankle was not in harmony with that attitude. She had taken only what the doctor prescribed in the immediate aftermath of the fall, the excellent gentleman having made the forgivable assumption that nobody in her right mind would attempt, next morning, to perform a show-jumping round at the country's premier equestrian event with an ankle the size of a football. 'Like Rachel Hunt, I had to get permission to ride from the ground jury, the dressage judges to whom one has to appeal in those circumstances. I had to obtain permission to ride without a high boot, as I couldn't move the foot enough to get it in there: they allowed me to wear a little jodhpur boot, which is ankle-high, and for cosmetic event I wound a black tail-bandage round my calf. The judges know damned well we wouldn't ride if we weren't up to it, so the decision is pretty much left to us.'

On the Saturday night, however, Ginny was not riding, and no-one had the slightest intention of letting her get on a horse the next day. The decision was not taken until she had steeled herself to do a practice jump, which was some ten minutes before she was due to jump. Ginny alone took that crucial decision: she was prepared to go for it, so only one question remained — what about the horse?

Master Craftsman rose to the occasion magnificently. Murphy, not having completed the cross-country, was not allowed to show-jump, so much rested on the shoulders of a particular animal. 'He sensed,' says Ginny, 'that the old bag wasn't quite herself, and I think he genuinely tried to help. It was a fairly unorthodox show-jumping round, I have to admit, and not the style by which I would like to be remembered. But at the end of the day we went clear, and amazingly enough it gave us third place.'

A new meaning to 'give me a leg up'.

'Have I ever been plastered before? . . . well . . .'

That notorious pride apart, there was one other overriding reason to defy pain and go for broke on Master Craftsman — the silver horse. 'It was asking rather a lot of a young horse, of course, and I didn't really feel I was being a great help, but maybe they're better off without your help! I didn't honestly think the horse was going to suffer unnecessarily, unless I made the most fearful botch of it and had ten fences down, which would have earned him an undeserved reputation as a poor show-jumper. If I did miss my jerk, I knew he would get me out of trouble, so I thought it was worth a crack. Also I so wanted him to have one of those silver horses. That's *really* why I show-jumped, without the shadow of a doubt. Who knows, he might not get another chance, and why the hell shouldn't he get his after his tremendous performance on the cross-country? Now he has it, and his name will go on it: if I'd ended up twelfth I couldn't have cared less, just as long as he got it. Those silver horses mean so much . . .'

'My odd horse-shoe.'

'Crafty took me round and became my Olympic horse.'

CHAPTER FOUR:

HORSE SENSE AND A BIT OF HORSE TRADING

Once the competition at Badminton 1988 was out of the way, Virginia Leng had one clear object in mind: getting plastered. First of all, in the best possible sense: as will become even clearer later on, three-day event riders are no different from the rest of us when it comes to letting the hair down after a big occasion. 'Every Badminton,' enthuses the local heroine, 'we have a big party at Ivyleaze on the Sunday night, to which we invite everybody who's at a loose end. So we end up with thirty or forty people, and order smoked salmon and a huge turkey; lots of friends bring puddings, and cheese, and wine. If you've had a bad go at Badminton, you can get absolutely sloshed and it doesn't matter — and if you've had a good go, you can get absolutely sloshed and that doesn't matter either! It's a ritual we go through every year, even if we're not competing. The year the thing was cancelled, on the Saturday, which would have been cross-country day, we had luncheon here for thirty people — it was, ironically, a brilliantly sunny day. That's the only reason I enjoy Badminton — the party on the Sunday night . . .'

Not quite the only reason, for after Sunday night, comes, as regularly as a Holgate horse round a cross-country course, Monday morning, which is genuinely the team's favourite part of the annual Badminton occasion. Heather, Dot and Ginny rise late — in relative terms — and do absolutely nothing: crawl into the conservatory, have brunch, look at the video — 'We spend the day as complete slobs, because you are absolutely wiped out by what has gone before. Not so much physically, but mentally. Mind you, it wasn't like that in 1988 — I really missed out!'

Despite the joy of Crafty's performance, after all, defeat and some despondency were, for Virginia Leng, the consequences of Badminton 1988. The event was to prompt some soul-searching, and no little stocktaking on the part of Britain's finest equestrian competitor. She had an Olympic horse, thanks to Master Craftsman's new-found maturity, but did the horse have an Olympic rider? And what of the enigmatic Murphy Himself, so boundlessly talented, but with a talent for stepping out of bounds? It was time to reflect on a host of issues raised — as is the case in any sport — by one of three-day eventing's major gatherings.

What was Badminton's place, after all, in the great scheme of equine things in this Olympic year? Had the course been too severe a test of horse and rider, given that for once Badminton was not an end in itself, but one of the means to a gold medal end? 'The policy,' reflects our central character, 'is that in an Olympic year you don't want just to finish off your Olympic horses, or indeed anybody that might be a contender for an Olympic place. The idea is that Badminton is then used as a form of first Olympic trial, in one sense to confirm the old codgers like Ian Stark and myself, but also to try and find some new talent.

'Looking at it that way, if you make Badminton too difficult, you may wipe out some of those possibles — if not the whole team. In fact a lot of countries won't bring their competitors to Badminton in an Olympic year because they are worried about doing that very thing. Charisma, for example, wasn't brought to Badminton last year by Mark Todd — he did something amazing like only four horse trials before the Games. The Americans built a very, very big course in Kentucky for an event the week before Badminton, and ended up doing what we were always frightened of doing — getting rid, in one fell swoop, of most of their most talented horses and riders. The course was too big, with no alternative routes, so everyone had to go the big way, and the consequence was big trouble. They were trying in some ways to go along the way of the British. They hadn't had major success, in places like Gawler and so on, but sadly for them they went over the top in their search for a better way of going about it.'

On the other hand, the scale of the Badminton challenge throws into relief the achievement of Ian Stark, and helps Virginia, by contrast, explain what happened to her. 'Ian, in one sense, was in a strong position when he went to Badminton in 1988. He had a horse, in Sir Wattie, which had already won it, and another, Glenburnie, which had shown a lot of talent by going very well at Burghley. Also he's a very good competitor, and his confidence was high. So much so, we had almost assumed he was going to win, he was on the kind of high that was going to roll along until the Olympic Games. In the betting which people can indulge in at Badminton, he was favourite — but to finish first and second was really something rather special, and that hadn't been done before. And I doubt very much that it will be repeated in a hurry.'

Looking back on Badminton 1988, in fact, and leaving her own achievement behind, Ginny Leng was able to highlight the contrasting fortunes of three-day eventing in another way.

At the end of the dressage, a competitor named Rodney Powell was in a strong position on his horse The Irishman II. 'Looking good at that stage,' is how Ginny remembers it, 'but two stops at fence four soon turned that around. The aim for Rodney was the Olympic Games, he was totally homed in on that one objective — and basically he blew it. He actually messed up one of the easiest fences on the course, and then did it again because of the sheer shock of having done it in the first place. Relaxed again for the show-jumping, by which time it's too late — and he was outside that coveted top twelve, his dreams of Seoul disappeared into thin air.' To underscore the point, there were, in the show-jumping, just sixteen clear rounds, which accounted for under thirty per cent of those who attempted the course.

How aware are the competitors of what other people are doing? It might be thought essential, in an Olympic selection trial, to keep a close watch on the opposition. 'After the dressage, I suppose, and after the cross-country, I have a quick look down the list to see how everybody's got on, but it's a very casual interest, rather than getting worked up by the other's marks. But I always make sure to have a good look on Saturday night, so as to be able to commiserate — or congratulate — at the vets' inspection on the Sunday.' In the midst of her own travails, in fact, Ginny spent an hour consoling Tinks Pottinger after her horse had failed the vets' inspection: the burning desire to compete need not extinguish the ability to show compassion.

True post-mortems, however, begin only when the event is completely over and done with, back in the comfort of home. Comfort? Not after this Badminton . . . Getting plastered, that was still the object of the exercise — but this time in the most literal sense. There was, after all, the small matter of a large ankle. After

'The Badminton Cocktail Party — a highlight I had to miss.'

Badminton, Ginny went straight to physiotherapist Mary Bromley for treatment. On to Bristol for X-rays, and plaster — the last thing Mary wanted. What to do? Keen to upset neither the doctor nor the physio, Ginny compromised by taking the plaster off, not after two-and-a-half weeks as recommended, but after a mere five days.

Her plan was to go to Breda to watch Ian Stark compete on her horse, given that she was unable to ride herself. By that time the swelling had gone down, and Mary Bromley was able to tell straight away that the ankle was dislocated. Manipulation took care of that complication, and the patient thought the worst was behind. Off to Breda, and enter Mr Stark on Virginia Leng's Ballyhack. 'Scottie' had already obliged by riding Ballyhack at a horse trial on the Tuesday after Badminton, flying down to help Ginny out of her predicament. He was happy with the horse, and

expenses were duly paid to get Ian to Breda to repeat the favour.

It was to prove a momentous meeting. Like Ginny, but for different reasons, Ian Stark was not in the position he would have liked to be in at that stage. His Badminton-winning horse, Sir Wattie, was fine but second-placed Glenburnie, for all his talent, was proving extremely brittle: a six-month lay-off for the animal was not what Ian would have hoped for to follow his unique achievement. Where Ginny's natural reaction to a major event like Badminton is hunger ('I just eat and eat and eat'), but not to get grouchy or difficult, Ian is prone to a form of post-natal depression. The loss, temporary or otherwise, of such an exceptional animal as Glenburnie was not designed to help his frame of mind. Horse trading, therefore, was in the air . . .

In Holland, Ginny went to a physiotherapist every day, still suffering severe

Crafty on his way to silver — a very well deserved silver horse that is.

pain, but as a relief from the other pain of not being able to ride she forced herself to hobble round the Breda cross-country course. 'Ian did a fantastic job,' she acknowledges, 'but because Mummy, Dot and I had time, which we normally don't have, the discussion turned to Murphy Himself. I was adamant that I wanted to qualify the

Ian's wonderful pair — Sir Wattie and Glenburnie.

horse for the Olympic Games. There were two choices: Bramham, or an event in Canada, both of which, because of entries and the usual administration, had to be decided within the next week. The whole point was, was I going to be fit enough?'

Not the whole point: other pressures intervened, from the most faithfully supportive area in Ginny's life. 'Mummy and Dot both put me on the spot. They were adamant that they would not come and watch me on that horse, and that was a sad state of affairs, as the whole point of my competing is that we should all be able to enjoy it together. What really frightened them, funnily enough, was that after the fall he tootled off, and if my foot had been caught . . . I agreed with them, too, on the fact that I had been on the borderline of control with that horse for so long, that at some point something was going to happen, and sure enough it did.'

As the discussion grew more heated, enter Mr Stark with the suggestion that they exchange Murphy Himself for Ian's horse Griffin. Curiously enough, there had been serious talk, three years earlier, of swapping Master Craftsman with Griffin at the novice stage. This had been vetoed by Heather, while Ginny was persuaded that Crafty was too big. Three years on, Ms Leng was unsure, and the offer from a Swiss gentleman of a great deal of money for Murphy prompted further taking of stock. Did she want to continue eventing? Answering herself in the affirmative, she wondered next what the state of her horses would be. A lot of money for Murphy would buy another horse, but not one of the stature, say, of Griffin.

The exchange became more appealing, and what followed was straight out of melodrama. 'It took place in the greatest secrecy at Weston Park,' laughs Virginia. 'Mrs Plant, the secretary there, is a great friend, so we rang and swore her to secrecy and asked permission to come and school the horses. So there was Mummy, Dot and I, and Murphy, with Mrs Plant; and Ian and his wife Jennie fetched up with Griffin, and we each eyed the other's horse carefully, as neither of us had really taken a long, hard look before! Next we got on board, and I was as nervous as a kitten — I hadn't ridden cross-country since Badminton, I wasn't sure how my ankle was going to behave, I was on a strange horse, and the responsibility of riding each other's horses over big fences was weighing on me.

'After all, we had to test them over advanced fences, otherwise what was the point? Funnily enough, Griffin ran out with me at the start, at a tiny fence, just as we were warming up. And it was a very good thing, as Ian told us he was a bit cheeky and liked to test people out. So

Horses for courses! — the switch completed — Griffin and Ginny . . .

we'd got that out of the way from the start, and the rest was a great success.'

The deed was done that very day, the horses going off to their new homes for ten days or so. Ian had been briefly to Ivyleaze to try Murphy in the school, which had not been a good idea as Murphy is rather boring at home, a little lackadaisical, and Ian's reaction was cool. The cross-country experience in Shropshire changed all that, however: no money changed hands, the sponsors were duly informed, and two happy riders left the scene.

What, then, is Ginny's feeling about Griffin? 'He's a very talented little horse, very careful, so I'll have to be cautious about not over-facing him too soon. Careful horses tend to be very cautious; the brave horse tends to be a little careless, so you have to watch what you are doing, whatever the horse's disposition. Badminton 1989, particularly as I don't know at this stage what the course will be like, may not be a good idea, though of course I shall enter him.'

In a sport where, clearly, the psychology of the horse is at least as important as the mental well-being of its rider, the other fascinating question was that of Murphy's reaction to his Badminton fall from grace. 'He was definitely a very different horse in the stable. He wouldn't come and put his head over the door, but stood at the back of the box. When we walked in, he didn't want to know. He sensed the huge disappointment, because the people's attitude towards him had changed. He was definitely on the depressed side; nobody, of course, had mistreated him in any way, but he wasn't getting the usual, 'Morning, Murphy, how are you?' He wasn't a happy horse . . .'

Given Ian Stark's plight, the acquisition of Murphy may be a boon. Ginny, who as reigning European Champion enjoyed the luxury of not *having* to go to Badminton in order to ensure her selection for this year's event at Burghley, could afford to let Griffin miss Badminton, whereas Ian would almost certainly have entered him. Ginny's reason for going to Badminton 1989 would be 'simply' to try and win Badminton, not with the aim of qualifying a horse for anything beyond that point. The build-up to Badminton, never short of savour, is made the more piquant by the delicious irony of watching these two great riders on horses which a short time ago were in different stables altogether.

The account of the great Salop horse-trading adventure would not be complete without Heather Holgate's version of events. Sensible enough at all times to allow her gifted daughter's talents to speak for themselves, and to trust Ginny's judgement, she found herself, thanks to Murphy Himself, in an invidious position. Professional detachment, in short, was in open conflict with a mother's natural and instinctive concern.

'My idea,' says Heather, 'was that swapping would be better than selling, as that would have left us short of advanced horses, especially as she had put so much work in with Murphy. It was a much easier decision for us to make than it was for her. So if we could take her mind off him, get it focused on another horse, that was much better for her than cash. And in any case you can't just go out and buy advanced horses.

'So what happened in Holland was simply a case of two and two making four. Scottie, we knew, was one of the few people who could ride Murphy Himself properly. He thought Griffin was a bit small for him, at that stage, but he had done well with him at Saumur, and obviously rated the horse. He's a very straight up-and-down person, Scottie, and sometimes an opportunity just comes along like that. Mind you, Jennie was very fond of Griffin, and he was sceptical, but it all turned out quite well.'

Heather's unease over Ginny and Murphy had existed since the horse was four, because even then she could see he was going to be too big for her. 'The first couple of seasons, he was difficult but manageable. Then, when he started taking off with her . . . Well, I worry enough as it is, without added strain, and as far as I was concerned Badminton was the final straw. On the other hand, it was desperately difficult for Ginny. I don't think Murphy cared very much what we thought of him, strangely enough: he's a big horse, he has that Irish temperament in his breeding which you can do nothing about. But he was the only horse Ginny has ever bought herself, and there was so much pride and time invested, and I thought it was an awful lot to ask her to give him up. But I just felt that one day he would probably kill her . . .'

Heather's lifetime of experience with horses shows in her straightforward analysis of Murphy's problem, when related to the relatively diminutive stature of her daughter. 'You can manage a tall horse, to a certain degree, that hasn't got a long back. But if he's got a long back, like Murphy, giving him all that scope — there isn't a fence in the world that would stop Murphy — then you cannot possibly get him together if you have short legs. As a rule, we try never to buy horses like that, and Murphy wasn't big when Ginny acquired him — that's just one of the pecularities of Irish horses.

'This is a very dangerous sport anyway, when everything is going as well as you can possibly get it going. It's rather like being in a racing car without suitable brakes on it: as Ginny found, you can never let that car go faster than the speed within which you're capable of braking. She had to ride Murphy like that. In the first place it wasn't doing her riding any good, as he was pulling her forward constantly; and given time I think she probably would have lost her nerve, because you can't go on under those conditions and ride well. If you haven't got

confidence, you may as well not start. And riding a horse, you *do* get an uncanny feel for the slightest thing . . .'

Pride, however, is not the prerogative of Holgate Jr alone, for Heather issued a very clear warning to the new owner of Murphy Himself. 'I told Scottie at Boekolo — which he won on Murphy while we were third on Griffin — that we would give him a year, but when 1990 comes, he'd better look out! And he had the good grace to agree.'

It would be unfair, surely, to deny Virginia Leng the last word on this sad result of her 1988 Badminton, for the motor racing analogy grinds to a halt when it comes to separating a rider from a horse she has cared for, schooled and known so long. A bond is being severed, and Ginny felt the pain of it as much as she felt the physical pain of her dislocated ankle.

'I felt he had really gone to perfection until we had our Badminton mishap,' is how she sums it up. 'I can only feel that he was telling me again he was going to get away from me somehow, and he took the opportunity when it arose. Being small, not as strong as a man, I have to accept those limitations: I am physically just not big enough for him. He is also very difficult to ride on the flat, because he has such big movement, and you need long legs to get the whole thing organised.

'I used to find him exhausting to ride: it was always such a big effort, I had to get myself mentally wound up to get on him each morning. He was a difficult, big horse, but I'm a stubborn little mule! Where he beat me was his physical strength against mine, which was unfortunate, but he certainly never beat me mentally . . .' Pride does come after a fall, then; but Virginia Leng, in the aftermath of her Badminton fall, was about to take another cruel knock in an Olympic year that seemed determined to turn sour on Britain's best medal prospect.

. . . Murphy Himself and Ian Stark. The future will be interesting!

A Day Out in London
20th April 1988

'It wasn't our fault.' With these words oft repeated in the next two hours, Ginny and her agent Judy Stott explained their late arrival at Peter Dazeley's photographic studio in Chelsea. Peter seemed untroubled by the 'excuse' and calmly organised his team.

The 'client' — Ebel Watches, one of Ginny's principal sponsors — arrived half an hour later with the timepieces and at 17:20 pictures began to be taken.

At 06:30 Ginny had exercised horses at her home in Badminton. At 08:30, attired for a business day, but carrying a further three changes of clothing, she drove her silver Porsche to London for a meeting at 10:30. A fruitful sartorial discussion with Viyella was followed by a scenic excursion to Whitechapel in east London, there to encounter Follett Cars, providers of the 'silver dream machine' which makes the hours spent travelling more stylishly comfortable — a different horsepower this. Photographed adorning the car whilst holding another business discussion, the other key protagonist was delayed and so was the all-important midday lunch. Late now, and in enough traffic to discourage even a patient London cabbie, the journey to Chelsea was a timetable breaker.

Emptying the car of three people — Ginny, Judy and Sarah — was an improbable exercise: Ginny had a wardrobe, Judy had crutches (a skiing legacy), and Sarah an armful of cameras. Add to this a saddle, tack and riding boots: it was hardly surprising that 'Lloyd' — a model horse from Bracknell — the patient and talented Sally and Gill whose manoeuvring of the horse box in the narrow mews had already accounted for Peter Dazeley's designer signpost, Hazel who made tea, produced cakes, with a lovely smile were all called upon to render rapid and appropriate assistance. Whilst the trappings were transported and the studio arranged, Ginny was seated in front of a mirror, tea in one hand and cigarette in the other, whilst Kit Campbell restored her face, and cajoled her hair into 'a vision of loveliness' — she *looked* terrific.

Aided by a much needed aspirin, the first 'shoot' was 'casual' — it took 20 minutes. Dressage uniform meant a change of watch and to the constant encouragement of 'Take a grip' 'Lloyd' competed with Ginny for 'enthusiasm' points from the attentive throng. The watches glistened in the light, and Judy's crutch earned its place in the day, when an orange rag was run up its length and waved at the ubiquitous Lloyd to ensure his attention to the flashing camera. Another change, another watch, antics with a bucket and general encouragement by all, guaranteed a lightly successful 'shoot'. Fiona Cochrane from Ebel smiled with all the pleasue of a happy client and Peter Dazeley orchestrated Ginny's now tired frame with all the skill of a pictorial masseur. Time to go home — it was 19:30. Badminton and bed were just two hours away . . . except that Ginny wasn't going home yet. A rapid reloading of the car, affectionate farewells to humans and 'Lloyd', and Ms Leng headed off to Stroud for a meeting with Captain Mark Phillips to discuss amongst other things her Great Ormond Street charity ride in June. The following morning Ginny was up at 06:00 to exercise her horses.

PS. Later in the year, Ebel Watches decided on a new sponsorship policy and sadly Virginia Leng's contract was not renewed.

Peter Dazeley in watchful mode.

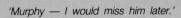
'Murphy — I would miss him later.'

CHAPTER FIVE

LOOKING FOR WAYS FORWARD

'Ballyhack: the first horse Ian "test drove" for me.'

Public personalities are a lot like people. Their lives, like ours, run not in straight, smooth lines, but in peaks and troughs, and 1988 was adding more of the latter to the life of Virginia Leng than of the former. After the fall at Badminton, and after Murphy's fall from grace, came a fall of a different, more personal nature: the breakdown of her marriage to Hamish Leng.

Hamish had equestrian connections himself, in the sense that he is the son of General Sir Peter Leng, chairman of the Racecourse Association, and is a successful financial consultant. Though he supported her at major equestrian events, theirs, by Ginny's own admission, was no conventional marriage. Their honeymoon, three years before, had set the tone, when they played elephant polo in Nepal . . . And theirs was a coming-together of two people with exceptionally busy lives, where time was not always theirs to give to each other.

'In simple terms,' explains Virginia herself, 'we were two terribly busy people.

What is extraordinary is that you can be good friends, the best possible friends and actually love each other, but cannot live together as what is usually taken to represent a married couple. That's basically what our problem was, and it is as simple as that. Our decision to part was something we arrived at over a long period of time, rather than something that happened as a bolt out of the blue. We had taken a long time, and several routes, on the way to that decision. Then it was taken, and that was that.'

Personalities are a lot like people, too, in their ability to get on with life despite such regrettable failures. The happy consequence of their separation is that Ginny and Hamish Leng have rediscovered the friendship to which she refers. 'What's interesting, and deeply pleasing to me, is that we get on better now, and if I had a problem, I'd ring Hamish to talk about it tomorrow. And he comes for supper, or for lunch, drops in — it's really nice.' Where personalities are not like people is that their lives are lived in the public domain; it is remarkable that Virginia coped with the breaking of this news, took a deep breath, and pressed on with the year in question. The breakdown of her marriage was a new and deeply painful blow: what she had to do next was pick up the reins, get back on course and approach the next obstacle in the best shape she could muster.

The next obstacle, as it happened, was the Bramham international three-day event. 'It was the next step forward,' is how Ginny expresses it, turning back from personal considerations to the professional task in hand — a form of therapy, one is tempted to say, and who could blame her for that? 'The point of Bramham,' she goes on, 'was that now Murphy Himself was not qualified to go to Seoul, what were we going to do? Let's see, we thought, Beneficial is a good horse — let's find out how good. He's done a lot of advanced one-day events in the spring, Bramham was a qualifying event for Seoul, people were

being selected to go on the long list for the Olympic Games *from* Bramham, so let's give it a crack.'

The lady herself was very worried about riding at Bramham. She was still in considerable pain, and walking the course itself was a new and familiar nightmare. Physiotherapy was still the order of the day, and to add to it all Beneficial did something that scarcely furthered the Leng cause. 'Just before I got on him at the start of Phase A,' Ginny recalls with feeling, 'the bloody thing stood on my foot with a stud — the *other* foot. Have you seen those studs? They're quite big, to say the least, and I was hopping around in pain from one foot to the other. "This is all I need," was what was going through my mind, alongside the temptation just to laugh. After all, why bother?'

Confidence, in a word, was low — bear in mind that this was early June, less than a month after Badminton. But Beneficial, like Master Craftsman on a previous occasion, was equal to the task. 'He gave me a really good ride, and I felt good for lots of reasons: he'd coped quite well with the cross-country, but more importantly for me I'd ridden him quite well, I was on form. So I was able to feel that the Badminton fall hadn't perhaps taken everything away from me, and in that sense Bramham was rather an important competition for me.'

As it turned out, Ben had a show-jump fence down, but that was hardly the end of the world. The horse was put on the long list for Seoul, so one primary target had been well and truly hit. The thinking after Bramham was very positive, because Ginny had two horses on the list for Seoul, Master Craftsman and Beneficial. If anything, the only cloud on the horizon was the rider: not for any loss of ability, but because of the legacy of that ankle.

Typically of Virginia Leng, her own predicament was not uppermost in her thoughts, for she was concerned about riders who might well have expected to

70

With Beneficial results.

accompany her on the next quest for Olympic glory. One of these was Lucinda Green, six times a winner at Badminton. 'It was awful,' recalls Ginny. 'She was lying first, and then had all these fences down in the show-jumping (Lucinda ended the competition in fourth place). We were all longing for her to win, too . . .'

Bramham, then, was to Lucinda Green what Badminton had been to Ginny and Murphy — the last straw. 'She'd had a very tough year up to then, and at last everything was spot on for her, and as luck would have it, it all went wrong again. The one to take her place was Jane Thelwall, who won for the second year running on King's Jester — every cloud has a silver lining.' For Ginny, however, Bramham had proved a significant milestone. Beneficial was now a strong supporting player to Master Craftsman, who had earned the limelight at Badminton: there was, after all, a way forward.

As an escape from personal stress, there

'Oh, s . . . ugar: the team would miss Lucinda's sense of humour in Seoul.'

72

was also at this time an opportunity for Virginia Leng to exploit her celebrity status in the service of a different cause, and her work in that respect is given the separate treatment it deserves. In equestrian terms, however, the Olympic Games were looming ever larger on the calendar. The next step forward, as far as Ginny and her horses were concerned, was Holker Hall.

'This,' states Ginny simply, 'was the most important one-day event of the year. It was the final British Olympic selection trial, and as such assumed an importance that normally Holker Hall, for all its charm, would not enjoy.' Holker Hall is near Cark-in-Cartmel in Cumbria, a long trek for team and horses, Heather performing the usual heroics at the wheel of the lorry while Ginny geared up mentally for the event.

'The basic approach was to go there, stay on your four feet and put in a clear round. To win would be nice, of course, but that wasn't really the object of the exercise.'

Sir Wattie — his retirement after Seoul would leave Ian Stark in need of another top horse.

Henrietta Knight, in the chair on the Selection Committee, issued a clear instruction that the riders were to go at a comfortable speed across country, not slowly, but not flat out — why risk an injury to one of the horses at this late stage?

Nine short-listed riders faced the Holker Hall ordeal. The cream rose instantly to the top in the dressage, where Ian Stark and Sir Wattie led from V. Leng on Master Craftsman — 'an impressive test,' was the rider's summing-up, 'but I do wish he were a little more attentive.' Ninth at that point, and cast into considerable gloom as he surveyed the Seoul prospects, was one Captain Mark Phillips on Cartier, who had done a good test marred by mistakes that were purely the result of tension.

While Crafty had a show-jumping fence down — 'I could have kicked myself,' said Ginny — the cross-country section presented no major difficulties. Ian Stark duly secured a fine victory, and it is interesting to note that in the advanced class Scottie also chalked up his first significant win on a horse called . . . Murphy Himself. Virginia herself was reasonably reassured by an eventual sixth place. 'Of course the winner was given a great deal of useful publicity, and so on,' she recalls, 'but he hadn't gone out hell-for-leather to win — that isn't the point of the final trial. It's a rather tricky event to size up, and the Press make rather a big deal about the placings, which I personally feel is not what they should be doing. We're there to do a job, get the horses round safely, and the results as such are irrelevant. You're not looking for a specific result, or out to prove a specific point, you're trying to maintain a reputation, and show that the horse is still looking good.'

The event also had its compensations. 'It was a beautiful day, one of the hottest of the summer. I was finished by lunchtime, having done my dressage the day before, and I lay flat out on the grass for the rest of the afternoon sunbathing. I was feeling both relieved and satisfied, and everyone else was thrilled even though we weren't in the first five. We had done the job we set out to do, so it was time to lick ice-cream and reflect on a successful weekend without heroic achievements.'

Not everyone could derive the same satisfaction from the long trip north. Jane Thelwall, a member of the team in Poland, had a fall and realised, like Rodney Powell, that Seoul selection was unlikely. 'We did a lot of sitting down and consoling,' adds Ginny. 'Mark Phillips and I sat on a straw bale in the middle of the field with Jane and urged her to think positively — forget the inevitable thoughts of not being good enough, set your sights on the next target. So what happens? She goes and wins Burghley, which was a very nice touch at the end of the season: we were all thrilled when the news came through to us in Seoul and sent her a "Told you so" telegram.'

The real test, in a sense, came the following morning. The riders concerned had a trot-up at seven in the morning to check on the horses' soundness, then there was The Big Meeting to decide who should be left off The List. 'We all had breakfast in the lorry,' Ginny remembers, 'and a very tense time it was. You've got all those riders there, and somebody's got to be left out, so it's rather nasty: two hours of sweat, basically. Then we were all called in collectively, told what was what, and it was time to exchange the usual congratulations and commiserations.'

The three team members were Ginny and Master Craftsman, Ian Stark and Sir Wattie, and — despite the gloom of the previous two days — Captain Mark Phillips and Cartier. Nominated as fourth member were Lorna Clarke and Fearliath Mor, and Karen Straker with Get Smart. At a later date it was announced that Ginny would also take Beneficial, who had gone so well at Bramham and in the events leading up to Holker Hall.

To counteract the tensions of the Cumbrian event, Ginny adds an amusing footnote to the trip, and one that takes a little of the gloss off so-called celebrity status. 'There was this little bed and breakfast where Lucinda had stayed for years and years, and I asked if this time I could also get in there. The dear old couple who ran the place had pictures of Lucinda everywhere, and copies of her books — she was their absolute heroine. As I was leaving, the lady said I ought really, she supposed, to sign her Visitors' Book as well, as Lucinda had done, because one day I might just be as famous as she was! So I took a deep breath, signed and left. It was very sweet when, a few months later, and having seen me in action in Seoul, they sent a postcard to apologise and asked me to come and stay again next year. It put me in my place good and proper . . .'

Last stop before the sights focused exclusively on Seoul was Rotherfield Park in Hampshire, where Ginny competed on Ballyhack and Griffin. No danger to her Olympic horses, then, but there was certainly some anxiety about their rider. It was a big course, so big in fact that the inexperienced Ballyhack did not attempt it. Griffin did, with two happy consequences: he and his rider formed, at last, a genuine partnership, giving Ginny great cause for optimism, but more importantly she had survived the event in one piece, and Korea beckoned. Lizzie Purbrick was the owner who collected all the silverware that day, a point to which the irrepressible Ms Leng drew some attention. 'Ah yes,' sighed the lady in question, 'but I would happily swap it all for a gong, and you're going to win one of those in Seoul.' Her confidence was fully justified, as it turned out — but only after further drama in the most dramatic competition of them all.

Holker Hall — the shortlisted team.

Kempton Park
29th June 1988

Arrangements for 'The Property World Olympic Race Evening' had been in the planning stage for a very long time. As the flat race fraternity welcomed the world of Eventing and Show Jumping and the beautifully manicured refugees from Henley added yet another social event to their champagne week, Kempton Park on the evening of 29th June 1988 was set to witness an inspired fund raising idea — at 19:15, in silks unfamiliar to the Equestrians, the calculating disciplines of Dressage, Cross Country and Show Jumping were to be abandoned in favour of the vigorous energetic sprint techniques needed to race on the flat for one mile and a furlong. The horses were different, the trainers were more cryptic and to look at the equestrian riders, you would think they had never ridden before. Walking the course with them simply exposed the acute level of nervousness being experienced. For Ginny the forecast was simple — the course was clockwise, which meant that her damaged ankle would not be able to withstand the pressures necessary to 'hold the rail' on the bend. Maureen Piggott had done it before, and she alone looked confident. Lucinda Green was only really concerned about finishing. Ginny wondered whether it was either possible or legal to be backed to come last. The starting stalls were not viewed with enthusiasm.

The changing rooms for the lady riders had been enlivened by the appearance of an unnamed male jockey clad, it was alleged, in only his crop — performance and appearance ratings varied.

Not surprisingly the regular flat race punters found the betting odds difficult to make sense of — a fact reflected by the long prices quoted at the start. It was a tentative but jovial group who assembled in the parade ring amidst the clicking cameras, proud owners and bemused equestrian enthusiasts. Armed with champagne glasses, smart member badges and huge numbers of computerised betting slips, the sponsors' boxes were packed to capacity, as the riders made their way to the start. In a gesture of lunatic good faith Ginny's agent, Judy Stott and her publisher backed her each way but the experts clearly fancied one of the men to win, with Mark Todd being especially singled out. They set off fast — too fast and the field was quickly spread. Then there was a faller — what kind of flat race was this! Rounding the turn it was impossible to pick the winner, but Maureen Piggott's quiet optimism began to look justified as she hit the front. However, Jane Holderness-Roddam on Mailman, looking every bit a champion jockey, stormed through to take victory as the greatest of all flat race jockeys' daughter eased up. And Ginny? Boxed in on the straight she found her horse had reserves, and forgetting her pre-race pessimism she took third as her agent leapt for joy, the richer by many pounds. Afterwards Maureen Piggott was fined £250 for 'failing to ride her mount' — in the circumstances an over zealous interpretation of the rules —

the money went to the fund. Mark Todd had to be helped to the weighing room in a state of sweated exhaustion and Ginny, faint from a combination of excitement and pre-race champagne was cuddled all the way to the dressing room by mesdames Stott and Gates (Citibank's sponsorship godmother). The champagne glasses were refilled and serious betting returned to the tote stands around the course.

Later, fed and watered, and the beneficiaries of a quite magnificent performance of marching and band music from the Welsh Guards and the pipes and drums of the 1st Battalion of Irish Guards, the excited mélange were treated to a superb firework display and a gun carriage exhibition by the Royal Horse Artillery. To crown the evening, the cannons and fireworks in perfect harmony gave a noisy but lustrous tint to the 1812 Overture.

The evening raised £50,000 for the British Olympic Fund. It was a triumph for Arlington's painstaking and professional team, and for the Eventing and Show Jumping riders an occasion which they all seemed more than happy to repeat. A different sort of riding, of course, but these are competitive people — each of them wanted to win. For Ginny, the long walk/limp around the course before the race was as serious an inspection as any made at a Cross Country course. It also revealed that for all her extrovert behaviour she had reached a time in the year when some of the difficulties caused by her very heavy training

schedule, the high mileage travel programme of Trials and Events, the need to fulfil the pleasurable but at times, time-consuming interests of her personal and Team sponsors, and the reality of her split with her husband Hamish, had begun to be evident. At Kempton Park, Dot Willis, keeping an eye, simply remarked, 'she's doing too much.'

Cary Brett-Holt of Arlington Securities was very pleased at the reaction and evident enjoyment of those present. It had certainly made the 2½ years' preparation and long hours 'in committee' with the BEF, Kempton Park and The Jockey Club, seem less onerous than had, in all probability, been the reality. It had been a chance remark from Malcolm Wallace to Arlington boss Raymond Mold which had sparked the idea, following the performance of the then Princess Anne at a flat race at Sandown. 'I had little idea that so much would be involved,' said Mr Mold, 'but apart from its enabling us to acknowledge the help and support of our clients and guests, I was very pleased to be involved in a project which not only gave pleasure to the equestrian fraternity, but also some tangible assistance to our Olympic effort. My best way of saying thank you to everyone is to say that I have already agreed to repeat the exercise in four years' time!' And Ms Leng? There were clear signs that she was beginning to doubt whether she would be at Seoul, let alone Barcelona.

The Wishing Well Appeal
FOR THE REDEVELOPMENT OF
Great Ormond Street Children's Hospital

49 Great Ormond Street, London WC1N 3HZ
Telephone: 01-430 1768 Fax: 01-831 1938

Patrons: Their Royal Highnesses the Prince and Princess of Wales

Help
Great Ormond Street
get better.

VIRGINIA LENG AND HER HORSES ARE HELPING GREAT ORMOND STREET

Please reply to:

Virginia Leng's historic ride from Avebury in Wiltshire to The Great Ormond Street Children's Hospital in London on 8th, 9th, 10th, 11th and 12th June, is fast gathering momentum.

She is being joined by sponsored riders all helping to raise more funds towards the £30 million The Hospital so badly needs for its rebuilding programme.

At the start in Avebury at 9.30 a.m., there are already 100 riders, and they will be accompanied by 4 trumpeters from The Royal Scots Dragoon Guards for a short distance along the Ridgeway. Steve Cauthen, John Francome and Willie Carson are participating on one of the first two days, together with an 11 year old ex-patient of The Hospital, who was successfully treated at birth for open heart surgery. Lunch on Wednesday is at The Shepherds Rest, Foxhill, Wanborough, Nr. Swindon.

There are in the region of 50 riders for Thursday and Friday with Stan Mellor's wife Elaine, and their jockey daughters Linda and Dana and Marcus Armytage the racing correspondent. Lunch on Thursday is on top of a hill 1 mile north of West Ilsley village, kindly carried there by the landlady of The Harrow pub. Lord Oaksey will be at lunch on both Wednesday and Thursday. On Friday, lunch will be held at The White Hart in Sonning-on-Thames.

On Saturday, for the ride through Windsor Great Park, when Ginny will be on her 1984 Olympic horse Priceless, tickets have to be applied for from Jane Irwin, Organiser of The Ride, and they are limited to 50. The lunch will be at Smith's Lawn, tickets also to be applied for, and then Ginny will lead HRH The Prince of Wales onto the Polo Ground. Among the sponsored riders this day will be a Great Ormond Street nurse, who has been given the day off, and Hannah Dowling, aged 3 years, on her pony Sooty, an ex-patient who was operated on successfully in 1987 with a kidney transplant.

On Sunday morning Ginny leaves Knightsbridge Barracks at 10.00 a.m. accompanied by 2 members of The Household Cavalry, Metropolitan Mounted Police, and members of the Civil Service Riding Club, and the Hyde Park Riding Club. They will progress to Marble Arch, Oxford Street, and on to Great Ormond Street. At the hospital, Ginny will be welcomed by Field Marshal, The Lord Bramall, KCB, OBE, MC. JP., Lord Lieutenant of Greater London, and Lady Bramall, and Colonel Sir Hugh Brassey, KCVO, OBE, MC., Lord Lieutenant of Wilts, and Lady Brassey, and other organisers of The Ride and the Appeal. All the children that are fit enough will watch from the balcony and Ginny will then visit the wards.

Further Details: Kim Cobbold 0249 812303, Jane Irwin 0380 850240
Jim Gilmore 0666 82 3335

CHAPTER SIX

WISHING WELL
AND WELL WISHERS

'Horses are helping Great Ormond Street, are you?
Join Virginia Leng
Wiltshire to London 8th-12th June 1988'

So proclaimed the leaflet inviting sponsors to support Ginny's efforts to raise money for one of the Nation's most publicised and most affectionate causes.

Famous people are inevitably persuaded to adopt causes, to help those 'less fortunate'. It is not a process deserving of scorn, but that tends to be the reaction because it is seen as a process devoid of genuine commitment. Emma Strange is a name unknown to most of the equestrian fraternity. For Ginny and those close to her, Emma was a human being whose presence did much to alter perspectives. She was a little girl whose cancerous body was finally deprived of life during the Seoul Olympic Games.

The full story of Ginny's relationship with Emma and the way in which her simple courage affected Ginny is not for this book, but the Ormond Street ride, and the media's reflection of the response it engendered is an integral part of Virginia Leng's 1988.

'Ian Botham is a "baddie" — a lovely chunky baddie. When he does something good he gets the world's attention and when he does something bad he gets the same treatment. I am a "goodie" — I have never taken a swipe at "PA" (Princess Anne) and I don't have a reputation for being "copy" for the world's press outside my achievements in Eventing.' This was

not a bitter statement from Ginny Leng but it provided a context for the way in which the Ivyleaze team's efforts — 'a slightly mad idea' — to raise money for Ormond Street were reviewed in hindsight.

'She was dying when we first saw her — as good as dead. Jaundiced, yellow, no hair and a body like a skeleton.' This was Ginny and Dot Willis' view of Emma Strange when they met her at the Bristol Hospital for Sick Children. It had been a request from Brough Scott that Ginny send a postcard to 'a very ill little girl' which had started the relationship, and a promise from Ginny that she could ride Murphy at Ivyleaze which gave Emma the will to do just that a month later — a feat which confounded everyone. 'Pretty special,' said Ginny. Jane Irwin, local organiser of the 'Wishing Well Appeal' wrote to Ginny to ask her for help — 'a display perhaps or a ride.' 'I decided to put my so-called celebrity status to good use and offered to ride from Wiltshire to London — do a Botham,' said Ginny, adding 'without really thinking about what would be involved.' The nodding of Dot's and Heather's heads and the watery smiles which accompanied their assent gave a firm indication of the enormous logistical problems which had had to be identified and later overcome during the course of a journey which had begun painfully on 8th

June just two days after the traumas of Bramham.

The idea was a simple one — Ginny would ride, sponsored by as many individuals and organisations as could be found, and in different parts of the journey other riders would join in (also acting as sponsoring vehicles) whilst workers and walkers would rattle buckets at passers-by to swell the coffers and generally attract attention. Mundane matters such as stabling, feeding, washing, attracting media interest, getting the Eventing world to add support, planning the route, liaising with the police, printing and distributing sponsor forms, selling sweatshirts, finding farriers, arranging interviews, fending off 'nutters', interrupting the polo at Windsor and riding down Oxford Street in London to the hospital, were just details!

Roads and Tracks to London.

On Wednesday 8th at 09:30 Avebury saw the start and hopes were high. However, doubts began to set in when firstly it appeared that sponsorship would fall way short of the original target of £50,000 and when, later, it emerged that many who might have been expected to add support, and particularly those from the top levels of the sport were not to be seen. 'We were depressed,' reflected Ginny, 'somehow because I wasn't a Botham I didn't seem to be getting the help I felt the idea merited, and particularly from many of my Eventing colleagues but also from the media.' Dot was more sanguine then and later. 'I felt that if we raised even half our original target we should be pleased to have helped at all.' It was Dot's pragmatism which made the whole team feel better. 'She was right of course,' said Ginny, 'it wasn't as if we were the only people raising money for Ormond Street.' Ginny also felt a responsibility to Jane Irwin and her team; 'they were fantastic — the hard core of a dozen simply never stopped and they smiled and they worked the whole time. I may have been the "celebrity" rider but they were the stars.'

The first part of the journey was the

'All along, down along, out along . . .'

Charitable cavalry.

'Yes, £50,000 . . .'

With Jane Irwin . . . ready for refreshments.

Roundheads and Bucketeers . . .

'Feted and patted'.

Ginny and Emma.

Rural Ride — Avebury to Charlbury Hill then to Little Hinton and Wantage. On Thursday it was the Ridgeway Crossing and on to Goring. Friday saw lunch at Sonning and then a gentle walk through to Hawthorn Hill. The pace had been slow, the response low-key and the weather unfriendly. A final target of just £15,000 had been set: 'Still a good sum,' said Dot.

The fourth day of the ride did not excite the pulse either — they had made it as far as Smith's Lawn, Windsor, but there did not seem to be anyone there to appreciate it. It was also cold verging on cold and wet.

The offer to shave her head, made on Breakfast TV, in return for £10,000 for Great Ormond Street, had not yet found a taker and Ginny's offer to 'streak' across the Polo lawn for £25,000 was, sadly, made to just a few friends — as her publisher didn't have the money, and the other males present had clear vision problems (not induced they claimed by alcohol) and Heather and Dot looked bored, this latest brand of prankery was not given the support it deserved. It could be that the cold weather assisted the decision. The plan for the day was straightforward enough — a sponsored lunch, a question and answer session and then a ceremonial — leading out the Polo teams.

The lunch in a marquee well away from the central hospitality area turned out to be rather more fun than at first seemed likely. The audience was a real mixture — from junior riders to reporters, from the chef d'équipe Lord Patrick Beresford to equine helpers, from fans and friends to officials, the 60 or so who took wine with the Ivyleaze 'sisterhood' certainly got value for money with some interesting answers to a variety of questions:

— Flying is easier for horses than driving
  — planes tend not to swerve — Heather
— The horse's temperament is the most critical factor in determining suitability for Olympic places — Ginny
— 70% of a horse's success is training — Heather

Top table at Windsor Park lunch — Heather, Dot, Ginny, Lord Patrick Beresford.

— Mares are OK . . . but never chosen — Ginny & Heather
— Ginny is superstitious — she always wears the odd socks acquired when aged 16 and the black silk she 'won' at the LA Olympics — Ginny
— Ginny was a pony club failure and a 'bad pupil' — Ginny
— Team spirit is Great Britain's victory factor at the Olympics — Ginny
— British riders don't ride other team members' horses — the responsibility is too great — the whole panel!

Once the top table had answered everything and ever conscious of time and money, an auction took place — a cake raised £130, a day with Ginny at Ivyleaze was won after exciting bidding by Equestrian photographer Gipsy Joe and Test Match tickets for Lord's were acquired for £80 (in view of the result one can only hope they went to a couple of Carribeans). All jokes seemed to involve Mike Gatting's much publicised exploits and by the time John Jason, Chairman and Owner of The Follett Car Group 'bought' the trip to Ivyleaze for 35 youngsters at a cost of £1,500, a total of £3,000 had been added to the Ormond Street coffers. At last there were signs of financial life.

The 'parade' on the lawn preceded a Polo match in which HRH The Prince of Wales demonstrated that he is a very accomplished rider and an even more accomplished quick change artist — that very morning he had Trooped the Colour with the Queen.

'The only embarrassing moment came when Priceless stopped behind the Band, lifted his tail and deposited his breakfast right in front of the Polo teams,' recalled Ginny with the same sense of mischief her famous horse had displayed.

The temperature didn't increase — neither did the crowd and there was justifiable depression at the small level of support. 'Nobody wanted to give us money,' said Ginny. Back in the lorry detailed discussions took place about the best route to the Knightsbrige barracks — starting point for the last stage of the ride the following day. Many of the ride's supporters and organisers also commented on the lack of interest displayed by other top riders and no doubt this was articulated further at dinner that night. Five circuits of the Great Park covered the miles needed to make up the distance from Windsor to London, and the final stage was ready.

London on Sundays starts slowly and late. Not so the Virginia Leng Citibank lorry — ensconced in the barracks by 08:00 and having avoided the debris of a colossal two car shunt at the top of Exhibition Road, Heather had ignored the 'Park Closed' signs at the entrance to Hyde Park and with the same thoroughness as always, had readied and steadied the team for the ride through the West End to the hospital.

Resplendent in their purple jumpers and with a vigour which had been absent the day before, the 'crew' got ready — a troop of Blues and Royals left the barracks and half an hour later Ginny left too — flanked by two soldiers from the Household Cavalry in full regalia, their sabres glinting in the early morning sun, and led with firmness by two mounted policemen, the five-horse ensemble crossed into the park, surrounded by bucket-swirling money gatherers and followed by a small cavalcade of cars. Hyde Park joggers, tourists and those with monstrous hangovers were relieved of their small change in increasing numbers. A brief stop at Speakers Corner which deterred not for one second the spokesperson for the 'gay-rights-for-unborn-babies' party from delivering his/her interminable message of gloom: the buckets, heavier by the minute, sounded a metallic message of hope for the children of Ormond Street. Into Oxford Street, raiding parties boarded buses, stopped cars and conveyed their simple and direct demands to the myriad of bemused and at times quite disagreeable victims. Traffic was held, the cavalcade parted, the buckets rattled louder — this was the last stage of the journey. As early Sunday drivers were forced to pull money from trousers with inaccessible pockets, the scowls of some were more than compensated for by the generosity of others. And so onwards across Tottenham Court Road to the hospital.

Great Ormond Street Hospital is an ideal setting for a reception committee — set back from the road with a drive of approximately 50 metres, the hospital buildings shroud the drive in a gentle U shape, with balconies and walkways running from one side to the other. A vantage point was no difficulty, a fact which was majestically obvious as Ginny and her male outriders turned in to face the climax of her ride.

To colossal cheers from a huge contingent of nurses and children, cleaners, parents, doctors, supporters and photographers, the last few yards of the journey were alive with the sounds of congratulation from the balconies to the steps in front of the main entrance. Children in wheelchairs, children carried by loving nurses and parents and children with pale faces provided a tapestry of life and colour which moved everyone privileged to share the moment. The horses were feted and patted, Ginny was feted and patted, cheques and coins were added to bucketeers' coffers. A firm and direct message of welcome was delivered in the sun by a grateful host before the tour of the wards and a well-earned lunch was taken in the place which provides so much for so many.

The ride had had its high spots and its low moments — there had been times when the Ivyleaze team had wondered whether the idea had been worth the effort. For some like Jane Irwin, Organiser, Press Officer, bucket rattler, cajoler and tireless enthusiast — the adventure had kept her awake at night, wakened her in the small hours, worried her and fatigued her — the moment of pleasure was also one of sadness, the show was over. The £60,000 raised was in the end far more than anyone had expected, especially after such an inauspicious start, and some of Ginny's Eventing colleagues did send 'generous cheques'.

'Team spirit is the victory factor,' Ginny had said in another context. No-one involved in the ride to Great Ormond Street disagreed. Afterwards just *The Times* carried a picture.

Reflecting on the whole event brought out a sense of pride from the Holgate team — 'it *was* a mad idea but I had proved to myself that I could use my "status" to help. I had also learned that other people could give so much more than I could,' said Ginny. 'Emma had been an inspiration to all of us and we had achieved something for her and for others like her,' said Dot. 'It was a fantastic experience,' said Heather, 'but I do wish that we could have had more support.'

Emma Strange died before Ginny Leng won her Olympic bronze medal. 'We really hoped she would last to the end of the Games but it was not to be,' said Dot. The sadness for all of them was manifest in her tone. 'Emma's legacy is the obvious one,' said Ginny, 'we all realised just how lucky we are to be fit enough to do what we do. I also realised that although I am not a "baddie" I can do something to help others less fortunate.' There was no sentiment in this remark, nor was it delivered with a massive dose of self-congratulation. There was, however, an unmistakeable hint of self-discovery — not a feature reported in the press.

What a welcome.

Beneficial's benefit appearance

Virginia Leng, the Olympic three-day eventer, completing a five-day sponsored ride yesterday with a military escort — two men from the Household Cavalry rode with her for the last few miles into central London. Miss Leng, undertook the ride on her horse Beneficial to raise money for the Great Ormond Street Children's Hospital in London, which needs £30 million for a rebuilding programme. She expects to raise between £40,000 and £50,000 for the hospital's Wishing Well Appeal. Her ride began in Avebury, Wiltshire, on Wednesday, when she set off in similar military style, accompanied by four trumpeters from The Royal Scots Dragoon Guards.
(Photograph: Mark Pepper)

Thank you The Times *(PS. We swapped 'dirty' jokes all the way down Oxford Street).*

The Olympic Ball
13th July 1988

THE OLYMPIC BALL
13th JULY 1988

Yet another Olympic fund-raising event. Yet another journey for the Holgate Team, this time resplendent in high heels, satins, chiffons and silks — and sumptuous they all looked. Set amidst the pink and yellow marquees erected in the grounds of Waldridge Manor, the 500 or so glamorous inmates of the Eventing world, wined, dined, danced and chatted whilst the organisers extracted money for the fund with the usual methods of raffles and auctions. Speeches were few, but as ever for the celebrities the work of being visible and being accessible to the throng was important. It was after all the riders and the team that were being supported and the pay-back was the chance for the rich enthusiasts to mingle with the Olympic Seoul sisters (and brothers).

Of course the evening was fun but for Ginny it had been a working day. Horses from 0800-11.30, a photographic session for this book until lunch, phonecalls, journalist appointments to fix and reject, ordinary but urgent domestic chaos, and then the journey to Aylesbury.

Inspired by David Piggott of Follett Cars, much of the evening's conversation seemed to revolve around the merits or otherwise of wearing stockings or tights. The outcome shall remain a secret! On the other hand there was the 'business' of entertaining host Paul Cohen of Citibank Savings' very delightful guests — a pleasure certainly, because theirs is a committed and knowledgeable support for Ginny and the Team, but

inevitably much of the talk too concerned preparation for Seoul and of course the fitness of rider and horses. Hindered by Murphy's legacy, Ginny's dancing was slightly restrained by movement if not by intent. As the July summer rain beat down, adding more syncopation to the alternative music systems which thumped their rhythms, there was the added attraction of a long walk through the mud to the cars to start the journey back. By the time Ginny reached her 'carriage' any suggestion of glamorous tights and high heel shoes had disappeared in the squelching ground — good to soft? No, just soft. By the time they reached Ivyleaze it was 03:30. A few hours later another wet English July dawn saw Ginny aboard her horses. Was the Ball worth the effort? 'Oh yes, it was great for us all to get out and enjoy ourselves even if I did feel ghastly for most of the day after!'

There was no mistaking however, the tinge of sadness which had momentarily manifested itself the night before. 'Hamish is my ex-partner,' she reflected, having danced cheerfully with him.

CHAPTER SEVEN

SEOUL OBJECTIVE AND SOME SEOUL SEARCHING

The final weeks before the team left for Seoul were, of course, restful, relaxed, free of functions and an ideal way of winding down before the ultimate competition. Horse feathers: the last seven days before Seoul were an endless round of public appearances, planning and training with due attention to detail. There was an Open Day for the public at Badminton, where the British representatives were going through the process called 'Team Concentration' — better described by Dot Willis as Concentration Camp — while sponsors' dinners and other activities were crammed into an overloaded schedule.

'Concentration Camp' was, in fact, a great deal more fun than Dot's description would imply. It was a four-week period (because of quarantine regulations) spent at Badminton, during which the team members were able to school their mature horses in the various disciplines, calling on the services of such experienced teachers as Ferdi Eilberg and Pat Manning, Pat Burgess for show-jumping, and Jane Holderness-Roddam for cross-country. There was the added benefit of being able to watch one another in action and pool opinions and advice. Not only that, but Ginny and her team-mates were nicely cosseted as well. 'Three-course suppers prepared by Mandy Downes every night', she says gleefully, 'it was wonderful!'

If the purpose of 'Team Concentration' was exactly what it says, the purpose of open day was to help generate some of the £200,000 needed to send the equestrian competitors to Seoul, and to mount the military-scale operation required of a nation with medal-winning aspirations. How fortunate for the British competitors, then, that a military man was on hand to take some of the non-sporting strain off their shoulders.

'Wol' is the name, though Major Malcolm Wallace is a more accurate appellation for this former Commander of the King's Troop and the Royal Horse Artillery who is now Director General of the British Equestrian Federation and oversees all aspects of British equestrian trips abroad. His views on Ginny and the other members of the team — and hers of him — are essential to an understanding of the team spirit that Virginia Leng insists is the crucial factor in recent British success. 'Having seen her through her emerging years,' says Wol, I feel she is unsurpassed: there is no-one better to represent Great Britain in a good light.' With Wol playing the role of co-ordinator, his functions as official chef d'equipe had passed to Patrick, Lord Beresford, appointed by Henrietta Knight at the start of the four-year cycle leading up to the 1988 Olympic Games. Another military man: ex-Royal Horse Guards, ex-Guards Parachute Company, a keen and gifted polo player and huntsman — and a man who shared Malcolm Wallace's opinion of Virginia Leng. 'She is, first and foremost, a marvellous friend. I came into this not really knowing much about eventing at all, and I have leant on her a great deal. She has always had time to answer questions, which is one of her great gifts, and moreover her advice has always been objective — she has never simply said what might suit herself. Like Ian, Lucinda and Lorna, she sets an example as a team member. If we can do nothing else, I would want their dedication and team spirit to be passed on to the next generation, for without a doubt that is why we have won these team medals. Ginny has done so much for eventing, its sponsorship, and Britain — she must be the best ambassador we've got.'

Fulsome praise, and Virginia is quick to admit the debt she owes to such men's support. 'Wol has always been a great mate, and was very helpful and influential when I was first a member of the team. For one thing, he is a very, very funny man, and a great bloke. Patrick, again, I have known since I was seventeen. It was a difficult task, taking over from Malcolm, and until the Olympics he had succeeded superbly, winning every team and individual gold medal available. Team captain in a non-playing sense is, I suppose, the best way of summing up what he does for us, and we have to look to him for everything. Transport organiser, nanny, collector of trophies, the man to represent our collective views about a course or a given issue: a man of many parts! He's also got a great sense of humour: not as gregarious as Wol, maybe, but in his own way he is incredibly funny.'

So much for mutual admiration. Wol, however, had his reservations about the British team's medal prospects in Seoul. 'The eventers have to be considered very unlucky,' he opined, 'if they don't get a team and individual medal. They couldn't have done any better recently — their performance as a team is staggering. But don't expect too much of Ginny . . . Her team performance will, as usual, produce a medal-supporting role, but it is just too early to take chances to win an individual medal with Master Craftsman.' As a fore-

'Our Supporters Club — they were marvellous.'

Lorna Clarke and Royal Eventer
— denied the ride to Seoul at the
very last hurdle.

caster, Wol was to prove less reliable than Mrs Purbrick, and now was the time for Ginny and the other competing members of the team to get on that plane and show once more what they were made of.

Getting on a plane has become one of the more mundane activities in modern life, but getting horses on a plane is another kettle of fish, if the metaphor is not too mixed. There were seven of them to be safely shipped halfway around the world, and to meet schedules they had to set off from Ivyleaze at the ungodly hour of three in the morning. 'We saw the horses loaded on to the transporter, and I thought a few more hours in bed would be just the ticket,' says Ginny. But no sooner had head hit pillow than the telephone rang. The journey of several thousand miles had ended, temporarily, a mere mile or so down the road.

Royal Eventer, one of Lorna Clarke's prospective mounts, had gone berserk in the truck. Dot and Ginny were first on the scene. The horse had been taken off the lorry, but was shaken and grazed. 'It had simply lain down in there and refused to get up. Now this is a horse that had travelled thousands of miles in its life, and never before presented a problem. What to do?' There was, after all, an aircraft waiting. Telephoning Henrietta Knight proved unsuccessful, so veterinary surgeon Peter Scott-Dunn took the decision: Royal Eventer would be left behind. Unwilling to accept, at that stage, such a drastic solution, Ginny suggested that he be left off *that* transporter, but Heather would use *her* lorry to try and get the horse to the airport in time. In vain: Royal Eventer again tried to lie down in Heather's horse box, and the mission was aborted.

'What had happened, we think,' explains Ginny, 'is that the partitions in the transporter went right down to the floor. Royal Eventer had been used to being able to spread his feet, because most horse boxes have partitions that go only so far down. But the aircraft, too, had partitions that went all the way down, so the horse would have suffered the same claustrophobia. Isn't it sad? If that horse had gone to Seoul, Lorna might have ridden him, because her first horse Fearliath Mor wasn't quite right, nor was Mark's — Royal Eventer might have been perfectly all right had he got on the aircraft, Lorna would have ridden him and, who knows, we might have won a gold medal. What's so extraordinary is that a detail so small made such a *huge* difference: and you can imagine the state poor Lorna was in . . .'

The trip out to Seoul, for the competitors, was thankfully free of such upsets, but Virginia managed to make her own mark none the less. 'We were all down at the back of the aeroplane,' she recalls guiltily, 'but Captain Phillips, because of who he is, was politely told that there was a seat up front if he wished to avail himself of it. 'Bugger this,' thought I, and I stormed up to the sharp end to confront him. "Look here," I said, "this is all about team spirit, so you get yourself down the back with us." Next to him, of course, there was an empty seat . . . So I sat down, and was offered a drink: then I was asked if I would like lunch . . . And on it went, until I ended up spending the whole trip up front as well. Just the occasional look back to think, "Oh, they'll be all right," and that was it!'

The real problems began, of course, at the other end, when the papers were not quite what the local authorities were expecting. In common with millions of modern travellers, therefore, the members of the British equestrian team for the 1988 Olympic Games were left hanging about the airport — all, that is, except one.

'Mark was whisked away by the security people, and we thought we would be kind enough to take his suitcase for him and reunite them at the hotel. Then we spied this rather lonely-looking briefcase sitting there in the middle of the concourse. We were some distance away, but I thought it looked familiar, and sure enough it belonged to Captain Phillips. It must have been sitting there for about ten minutes, and no-one had bothered.' Next was the effort to get to the equestrian stables, for there was a natural desire to see how the horses were, especially in the light — or dark, as the case may be — of events en route to the airport at the other end. Enter, stage left, one of the memorable characters of Ginny's 1988 Olympics: the team driver, Mr Yu.

'We did expect communication prob- lems,' she muses, 'but we did also expect a driver with some knowledge of the local terrain. Not Mr Yu: he was entirely clue- less. We lost the lead driver, of course, and nearly had an accident when a section of dual carriageway went down to one lane, and Mr Yu left it slightly late to get over . . . But at last we got there to see the horses, though we weren't allowed into the quarantine area because we hadn't yet got our accreditation.'

The excellent Dot was on hand by this

The team in high spirits.

Ginny and mike.

time, though she herself had nowhere to go. Unable to get into the grooms' quarters, unable to get into the competitors' villages, unable to get into the family village because Heather herself was not yet in Korea, she was a soul in limbo who had managed to squeeze her way, temporarily, into grooms' accommodation. 'It was ten at night when we finally completed the epic journey to see the horses, and no-one had told us we needed our accreditation to do so. We didn't think they would have been that sharp on security so early in the proceedings, because we arrived there well ahead of the main body of competitors. Pointless trying to do anything there, so back into the buses we piled and set off for the Orympic Willagee — the only way we could get Mr Yu to understand where we wanted to go. Olympic Village? Not round here, sorry . . . Oh, Orympic Willagee: no problem, we go now!'

There were two drains on the Leng patience from this point on: 'endless "official" functions,' as she now recalls them, and queuing for everything, the first wait being at the Accreditation Centre for photographs, papers and all the paraphernalia of modern international sporting competition. Humour was never far from the surface, however. 'When we came out of there,' laughs Ginny, 'I spotted that Mark's badge proclaimed him to be Captain Mark Phillipa, and we all just cracked up.' The gentleman refused to put himself through the ordeal by queue again, and throughout the 1988 Olympic Games the official computers and scorers referred to a hybrid competitor with an 'a' on the end of his/her name.

It was, of course, just one more tax on the Captain's temper, for he had assumed, when grabbed by protective hands at the airport, that his baggage, briefcase included, would be taken with him. He was very relieved to hear that all was in good hands.

Next, the rooms: the Games, clearly, were going back to their origins, for Spartan was the politest way of putting it. There were ladies' and men's buildings. 'On one page,' comes another laugh, 'we were told the Committee had very kindly supplied 40,000 condoms for the athletes,

HRH The Princess Royal — as President of the FEI she had a Seoul objective too.

and on the next page it said unforeseen circumstances at the Asian Games had led to the decision to split the sexes in Seoul!' Dressage ladies and three-day event ladies were in the same apartment, so there was a fairly broad sweep of age groups to begin with. Two tables, television set, four chairs, a kettle (to star in a later incident) and some mugs were all that interrupted the clean lines of the accommodation. Lots of people to share two bathrooms, no carpets or mats, and none of the things deemed essential to gracious living on the other side of the world.

'The biggest shock of all,' adds our horrified heroine, 'was the paper sheets — just like the sort of thing you have in hospital. Cupboard space was so minuscule we literally lived out of our suitcases. Hot at night, at first, but as the Games went on it gradually got colder, and you had only one blanket; and every morning, faithfully at four, there was the muezzin calling the Islamic faithful to pre-Olympic prayer.'

Interjection from Heather: 'The funniest thing, when the temperature was around eighty-eight, was that — because it was winter in Korea — the central heating came on. Can you imagine what it was like in those rooms??' Hunger, by now, had begun to gnaw at Britain's equestrian elite. It was, after all, around a quarter to midnight. Off in search of the canteen they went. 'There were about seven different restaurants,' says Ginny, 'and at first the choice of food seemed reasonable, with salads and fruit and things, but that got gradually less appealing as time went on. And the *queues* were an absolute nightmare: three in the morning, four in the afternoon — it made not the slightest bit of difference, and that was quite the worst part of the 1988 Olympic Games as far as I was concerned.'

No point striking out in search of raw materials to cook up your own midnight feast, either — there were no utensils in which to cook it up. Nowhere just outside the Orympic Willagee to go and find some faster food: given the Leng penchant for the occasional tasty morsel, Seoul must have stressed the system to breaking point. Heather ('Muggins again') stepped nobly into the breach, by joining the Seoul Club, where the team could go for lunch and a swim — but this was only when strings were pulled after the competition itself, for in the period leading up to the eventing there simply was not time.

Nor did matters improve when the members of the team took themselves off to the equestrian headquarters. 'What was extraordinary,' comes the indignant memory, 'was that at the start we were not allowed to eat in the grooms' restaurant. For once in the history of this sport, the grooms actually had much better food than the riders, and we were literally drooling outside the door, panting at the windows — and they wouldn't let us in. Miles from anywhere, you must remember, no way of getting some food. Then we discovered we were supposed to pick up packed lunches from the Orympic Willagee, bring them to the equestrian park and eat them on the lawn — and there was this perfectly good restaurant in front of us! We kept forgetting to order the food a day ahead, as we were supposed to, but then the grooms turned up trumps — it was just like school, stuffing bread rolls and the odd tit-bit down their trousers to bring out to their starving friends!'

If one Seoul objective was food and its rapid acquisition, another was the defeat of a telephone system which seemed designed to drive the invading foreigner mad. 'They drove me potty,' says Ginny, much of whose life seems to be spent with one of the aforesaid instruments at her ear. 'We had to buy these special cards, and they'd run out in two seconds — particularly if you were phoning home to check on horses, you would have time to mouth a quick "Hello" and that was that.' There were 'phones where you could pay by credit card, but . . . the queues were enormous; there were very few where you could reverse the charges. Leave it to the world's most 'phone-conscious nation to sort things out.

'The American athletes had figured out a system whereby you could get away without paying at either end. The Koreans discovered this *monumental* telephone bill after the Games were over and actually sent it to the US Olympic federation — an astronomical amount of money, because of course the news had spread like wildfire and everyone got stuck into the 'phones. We'd cracked a system that threatened to turn into another nightmare!'

There were other compensations, of course. If Stalag Seoul was theoretically alcohol-free, British ingenuity soon scotched that. 'We had brought the odd couple of bottles,' grins Ginny, 'and Pimms became our number one beverage. We'd get fruit from the village, and make pitchers — we actually bought the lemonade — to sit and sip on our little balcony before setting off for our gourmet dinner. It was, all things considered, a very attractive site, with that main, glass building, and to be fair they were trying very hard to cater for such a mix of cultures they were bound to have problems. The local girls wore those beautiful dresses every day, and there was always the fact that you were spotting somebody famous, and the training facilities were very good: there were a host of good points, and it was great fun to be made to feel so important in an environment which we equestrian competitors are not accustomed to.'

All of the apartments in which athletes were housed had been temporarily vacated by Korean families, for whom Ginny and her team-mates left grateful letters and gifts. Heather's driver, Mr Chin, later wrote to her several times, but though Ginny had left a good bottle and other items for Mr Yu, no such missive was ever received. Probably just as well: in the first few days in Seoul, Ginny and companions were driven through twenty red lights, eight of them in one morning; went on a dinner outing which should have been a twenty-minute drive but took fifty, largely because the intrepid Mr Yu crossed the river not once but five times; and were driven full tilt down the wrong side of a motorway after the obligatory U-turn in the middle.

'He was a really crafty character,' is Ginny's summing-up. 'He couldn't drive into the Olympic Park, so we had to walk from our building to the restaurant, from there to the outside of the Park to pick him up, and we always allowed fifteen minutes. If there weren't many of us in the bus, he would stop and pick up people, and he was charging them the equivalent of two pounds — but what cheesed us off was that the more he stopped for fares, the later we were getting. At one point I got on board on my own, and I was in a rush. So we stop and pick this chap up in the middle of a traffic jam. I made encouraging noises, because I had to get to the horse park, and we were just about to go flying past when I screamed at Mr Yu. He was determined to deliver his paying fare to a local village first, and it took some more precious time to persuade him there would be dire consequences if the order of priorities was not reversed!'

'Endless "official" functions,' Ginny said at one point, but there were some light-hearted and memorable moments too. A BBC party, for one, on a houseboat hired for the evening. 'The food was unbelievable,' she recalls with her face lighting up. 'Huge prawns, smoked salmon, oysters, crispy duck — every conceivable kind of luscious thing. Well, the British athletes walked in, and with a swish of wings we all descended on this feast — despite our efforts to be polite and make small talk, we were so thrilled by the sight of it all it just disappeared! That was the evening when Wol, who is a brilliant mimic, had us all in fits with his Korean accent, too, and we all got rather jovial and silly . . .'

Silly? V. Leng was seen at one point in the tiger disguise of Korea's Olympic mascot, addressing all and sundry in the most interesting fashion, but the prize for the funniest idea of the night went to Karen Straker. 'At one point she was introduced to a Very Important Official, who was holding a glass of wine. "Would you mind holding mine," she asked, "while I fetch a chicken leg?" Back she came with two, and invited him to have one. As he was about to say "No thanks", she thrust the chicken leg in his mouth. There he was with a chicken leg in his mouth, a glass of wine in each hand — and she promptly introduced him to Captain Mark Phillips!'

There was, too, an Embassy party the following evening, just for the equestrian members of the team, which Ginny was particularly keen to attend. There was business to attend to first, however, and she almost missed the ball.

Paul Cohen of Citibank Savings with friends.

CHAPTER EIGHT:

A HORSE OF A DIFFERENT COLOUR

A short distance from home, as we saw, was enough for bad news to begin filtering back. Once the horses and their riders had arrived in Korea, however, bad news — in both senses of the term — kept coming over the long-distance wires. As an expectant British public settled down to its own orgy of Olympics-watching, the *Daily Mail* carried a half-page picture in which, disaster of disasters, Master Craftsman was alleged to have fallen to his knees, with the obvious consequences for the lady in the saddle. Hearts were in mouths: what could have gone wrong?

Only one thing was wrong: the report. The horse was in fact Beneficial, and the incident itself was nowhere near as dramatic as the sensationalist headline would have had its readers believe. 'We were on the practice show-jumping course, at a grid,' is the clear explanation from the rider in question, 'which is a series of fences in a line. Now you can have one fence, one non-jumping stride to another fence, and the same again; or you can do what we call a bounce — take off over the first fence, land and immediately take off again. Beneficial tried, in effect, to bounce a non-jumping stride combination. Obviously he had taken off far too early for the second jump and landed slap in the middle of it.'

What upset Ginny most about the inaccurate newspaper report was the suggestion that she and her horse had actually stopped. 'Stopping, to us, is almost worse than a fall — it's a form of disobedience, whereas if you fall your horse at least has tried to get you over the fence. To all of us, as a team, it was a major slur on our reputation that Master Craftsman — the wrong horse — was alleged to have tried to stop, and in so doing had fallen to his knees — the wrong account. It was, in my view, a stupid report, because it was inaccurate about a team horse. And they were there at the time to take the photograph: why didn't they come and ask what had happened, and get it right?'

Pride, in short, had been wounded, and justifiable indignation was the result. 'We, at that point, are trying to win a gold medal for Great Britain — and a British newspaper reports something totally inaccurate. Had it been an American newspaper, or French, so what? But at times like that you really need the Press on your side . . .' A toss of the Leng locks, and the matter is dismissed. There was, after all, the business of winning medals to attend to.

The Opening Ceremony at the 1988 Olympic Games left an indelible mark, after the inevitable wait for the march past to begin. 'It was an incredible experience to go through that tunnel into the Olympic Stadium itself: and when the flag was raised and the flame was lit, that was the most moving moment of all.' Not that there was time to enjoy it, for the equestrians in the team were scheduled to put in some hours on horseback that afternoon. Two people in particular were sweating out the final hours before what might be the biggest competition of their lives, for the decision on whether to make Lorna Clarke or Karen Straker the fourth member of the team had not yet been taken. It was Karen's birthday . . .

Monday brought the first phase of Olympic competition, the dressage. It also brought Virginia Leng to the very edge of panic. 'That, for me, was one of the most horrific moments of the whole event, the one point at which I started to get really rather over-excited about the whole thing.' The root of the problem lay in an impossibly crowded schedule for Ginny's day, compounded by the mesmerising geography of Seoul and South Korea. The first difficulty was getting to the scene of the steeplechase and cross-country course, Won Dang, which was about an hour and a half away.

'I asked Mummy and Dot to meet me at the East Gate. Not the original pick-up point, because I had decided the East Gate was much quicker to get to, both for them and for me. The appointed time was 07:30, and they didn't come, and they didn't come, and they didn't come . . . and I started to panic, thinking they didn't remember which gate to come to. I had no means of transport whatsoever, I was stuck.' Heather breaks in at this point: 'You knew we were doing our best to get to you, but of course in Seoul, if you made a wrong turn, you were another hour going the width of the average field.' The city must have made those rice paddies look like a piece of cake . . .

'Major panic,' Ginny resumes. 'They're lost, should I stay here, should I go and telephone, if I go and telephone they'll come past and I'll miss them: it was an absolute nightmare, my little blow of the fuse, which is actually rather unusual for me.' Eventually Dot and Heather turned up, the team went off to walk — in the pouring rain — the steeplechase course, drive the roads and tracks, and walk the cross-country course, some of whose fences had been amended on the eve of the competition.

Unwilling to risk the journey from Olympic Willagee to her horses again, Ginny stayed at the stables in order to be aboard Master Craftsman at 07:00 the following morning. Just over an hour later, her Olympic Games began in the dressage arena. 'Crafty did the best test we could possibly have asked for,' she said later. 'It was accurate, he was very good in his transitions and halts. The only criticism I'd make is that I perhaps didn't ask for enough on the second extended trot, and in the canter work he could have gone a touch more forward. But in this atmosphere, he couldn't possibly have gone better.' Virginia Leng and Master Craftsman lay third after the dressage, behind New Zealand's Mark Todd on the extraordinary Charisma, and West Germany's Claus Erhorn. Karen Straker, incidentally, had received the appropriate

The vet's inspection was critical.

98

birthday gift: representing her country for the first time in a major competition overseas, she lay ninth at the end of the dressage phase.

The next task was to get the horses and riders to Won Dang again, for the steeplechase, roads and tracks and cross-country. Straightforward enough: but enter, stage left once again, the intrepid Mr Yu, this time doing battle with . . . ice cream. 'We kept missing out on meals, you will recall, and one of the things we were starved of was ice cream. Now Korea had some ice creams which we thought were just great, so en route to Won Dang we made Mr Yu make an ice cream stop. Poor Mr Yu actually managed to drop the ball of ice cream off the cornet straight into his lap, and the same pair of trousers just happened to be put on for the next five days!'

Security at Won Dang was suddenly very tight, as the riders had arrived unexpectedly early to walk the course for a final time. There were all sorts of other details to attend to, as well, and the way this was done gave Ginny one of the happiest memories of her 1988 Olympic Games. It was, in a way, a Hen supper.

'Hen (Henrietta Knight) had gone off and organised a wonderful picnic, which was in effect our supper, over which we went through everything that was going to happen the next day. Were all the riders happy? Did everybody have stop watches? Were the spotters organised? These are the people who go and watch certain fences on the cross-country, to watch out for certain details and send information back, if necessary, to the ten-minute halt box. I remember it very clearly: we had cold roast lamb, French bread, cheese, pate, and apple tart: it was a very French supper. And wine, in her room in the Agriculture College.'

Olympic competition is a severe enough test of horse and rider without the accidents that befell the British team on the second day of their Seoul Games. The first involved Captain Mark Phillips, first of the British contingent to tackle the steeplechase, where Cartier was in fine form. Sadly the horse was unable to repeat the effort on the cross-country, for on the trot-up Cartier pulled a muscle and was eliminated — a distressing end to the Captain's first Olympics for sixteen years, and possibly his last international competition.

Another major consequence, of course, was that Cartier's demise put added pressure on the remaining members of the team. How would one of the more inexperienced members of that team cope: Master Craftsman? He faced an uphill task, not only in the shape of the Seoul course itself, but in coming very fresh to this major competition. 'It was a huge disadvantage, on reflection, not to have given him a proper run in the previous six weeks,' says Ginny. 'He was a very, very fresh horse, almost a crazy horse when he got on to the steeplechase course. Normally he's very settled, looks at the fences, sees his own stride and over we go. In Korea, he was almost galloping at them, as if to say "Let me get at it", which was just what I didn't want. I wanted him to be so calm and collected.

'When I started the cross-country, therefore, I knew I had something different on my hands. I was not sitting on the same horse I had sat on at Badminton. I had something else to deal with, but I was not entirely sure what that something else was.' She was almost spared the trouble of finding out, for at Fence 4 catastrophe beckoned. 'That's where we nearly went splat,' she recalls. 'I thought I was going, in fact I was gone. But that's when I discovered that, basically, Crafty was just not concentrating. He was slightly fazed by everything — the fact he hadn't run for weeks, he'd gone on a long trip, he'd been in a strange place for two weeks without doing anything. The whole combination of circumstances had rather got to the character of the young, willing but inexperienced horse that Master Craftsman was. And that is exactly the ride he gave me.'

FINISH
PHASE-B

Mark Phillips and Cartier 'in fine form in
the steeplechase'.

Those early alarms behind him, however, Crafty realised there was still some way to go and began acting in a much more grown-up fashion. When the pair of them came over the last fence, Dot Willis and the other British supporters on hand were not the only ones to give vent to their feelings. 'I was very relieved to finish, because I had had to deal with a horse I wasn't used to. I felt nothing but gratitude to Crafty, though, for really trying his best.'

There had been other concerns as well, apart from the test of Crafty's character. Karen Straker, going well on the cross-country herself, had suddenly come to grief when Get Smart caught a hind leg as he jumped off the bank at the second water jump. Although the youngster swiftly remounted and went on to complete the course, the instructions to Ian Stark and Ginny Leng were just as swiftly altered.

'Go as fast as you dare,' she had been told, but the priority was to jump a clear round rather than really go for it. Time faults ensued: 'I knew from a quarter of the way round that I was behind time, but there was part of the course towards the end where I knew, if I had a fresh horse, I could make up time if I needed to — and that's what we did. On the last quarter I picked up time because most of the difficult fences were out of the way. I knew all along I was going to have time faults, it was just a question of how many. But with one that hadn't got round, one that had had a fall, my orders were "For God's sake get a clear round", and I took it accordingly. No point in giving the nation a collective heart attack, was there?'

If the British were having their travails, they were as nothing compared to the plight of the defending Olympic champions. At the end of the cross-country day, only two teams failed to get round: the Japanese and the Americans, team gold medallists at their own Los Angeles Games, but paying the price for not having competed in a serious event since May. Top of the heap, at that stage, was Mark

'Korea was beautiful in parts.'

Todd on the sixteen-year-old Charisma — but Crafty, half his age and with almost none of his experience, had put his rider in second place.

'If Ben had been more experienced,' adds Ginny, 'he would in fact have been a better horse for that course. A horse with a "pony" stride was needed, and of course just such a horse went on to win it. That fourth fence had always worried me, too. The Won Dang Walls, fences 27 and 28 were sensibly changed, but I would question, looking back whether there shouldn't have been longer alternatives. I did not agree that the lowering of the rails into the first water was a good idea. But once Crafty had jumped the parallel at the top of the hill so brilliantly, I thought, "Why not jump the corners and save messing about on the long route?" He had a rubber Kimberwick, but I'm not sure it suited him on the day. I think he thought the first single rail was a corner, so he jumped off on all four feet to avoid running out. His tongue was over the bit, and he was perhaps re-acting to it, but once those initial hairy moments were behind us he was fine. As I say, nothing but gratitude.'

Well, perhaps something more. 'The second I went through the finishing flag, there was a sense of complete relief, as if months and years of anticipation and preparation were over at last — "Done it! Done it!! Done it!!!" A four-year programme, and you've seen it through: it's actually a very big moment, and most dramatic just as you go through that finish flag. Mummy was ready to grab the horse, Dot and everyone were really thrilled, and of course on the television interview I said something fairly typical about being in need of a stiff drink . . . and meant it.'

If the build-up to the cross-country is a time for team spirit and thoughts that are private to your team, once the ordeal is over the Olympic camaraderie comes to the surface, and for Ginny, feeling the sense of relief she did at that point, the end of the day, the post-mortems, the sharing of the experience with the other riders, all left a good taste in her mouth. She did not see any footage of her own performance, however, until she came back to England. With Ian Stark and Sir Wattie also responding brilliantly to changed team orders and occupying third place at the end of the day, the show-jumping was clearly going to provide the gripping finale the world expected. As Dot Willis remembers it, the day was again different from most others Crafty had experienced. 'The ground in the show-jumping arena was flat and dead, for a start. There was more atmosphere than on dressage day, mind you, but not as much as at Luhmuhlen or Los Angeles. Crafty was aware, certainly, that there was a sense of occasion, but nothing like Badminton.'

After the euphoria of the previous day, Ginny by her own admission was astounded to find herself in second place after the cross-country. 'What went through my mind, as we entered the show-jumping arena, was that I was asking a hell of a lot in looking for a clear round that day. I was being really greedy — but on the other hand, the horse was quite capable of doing it for me. On the one hand, I suppose, I was trying to prepare myself for disappointment, while secretly hoping it was going to be one of those marvellous days.'

No atmosphere? This was death or glory where one's country was concerned, and any self-respecting horse knows that as well as the human on top. 'It was a very long course,' adds Ginny, who had exercised Master Craftsman for half an hour or so, taking three fences very cleanly, the horse looking sharp. 'It didn't really suit him at all, and there was a lot of galloping between those fences. He was very much over-excited by what was happening. He went into the arena, looked up, and after that he never put his head anywhere else — which of course is the worst place for a horse's head to be if he is to jump in the correct style. He couldn't jump in a proper, rounded way, he was jumping hollow and flat. So after practice jumps that were better than ever before, he went into the Olympic arena and had two rails down.'

It all sounds matter-of-fact, the ultimate anti-climax. In fact the wildest extremes of emotion still awaited Ginny Leng, as the four-year programme approached its final moments both for teams and individual riders. 'Two fences down, no chance of staying in the medals, was all I could see. It was disappointing for the horse, because I thought he deserved a medal. I assumed, in fact, I had been pushed down to somewhere around eighth, it was a complete disaster — and of course I was even more concerned about the team's position, as two rails down is ten points, and that's a hell of a lot.'

Because of her practice jumping and the concentration on her own round, Ginny had not the faintest idea of the shape of the competition as a whole. 'Bad luck about the silver medal,' said someone, the sig-

A partnership blossoms in Korea.

Karen Straker — the team's baby put up a tigerish performance.

nificance of the remark not sinking in at the time as Ginny asked about the team. 'No problem, we've cracked the silver there all right,' came the reply, and relief flooded over the Leng frame — she hadn't blown it after all. She was then able to watch Ian Stark and Mark Todd do their show-jumping rounds, duly securing individual silver and gold respectively.

'It must have been a good ten minutes after my own round,' she recalls, 'that Jenny Loriston-Clarke came up to me and said, "Well done — I'm sorry about the silver, but isn't it nice to have a bronze?" So I said, "What *are* you talking about?" "The bronze, of course — you've won the bronze medal!" "But I didn't win the bronze" — and back and forth it went.' While Ginny was aware that Ian had taken silver, she did not realise what had happened immediately behind the Scot.

Claus Erhorn, she assumed, had gone clear and put the bronze beyond her and Crafty. 'Because when he finished, the crowd went berserk — he'd jumped a clear round, and clinched the gold team medal, was what I thought. In *fact*, he'd had a fence down: now that didn't matter as far as the team was concerned, he could afford that and still win the gold for the West Germans.' To add to the confusion, Wol had come along and told Jenny she was wrong, Ginny had *not* won bronze. Instant deflation, collective panic: what the hell was going on?

When boards and scores were checked, Erhorn — in fourth place behind Ginny, who then had her two rails down — had also incurred time faults. Team glory was his, the individual prize was Ginny's. 'It was the finest present anyone could have given me,' she beams. 'Absolutely wonderful — it had been such a disappointment to go, as I believed, from the silver medal position right down the list, then suddenly to discover we'd won the bronze.'

Stark contrast — the normally cheerful 'Scottie' feels Olympic tension.

Crafty on his way to the record books.

Virginia Leng had in fact become the first equestrian competitor to win two team and two individual medals in two Olympic Games. From the debacle of that *Daily Mail* report, to the feeling of being on a strange horse over that testing cross-country course, to the despair of those fallen rails in the final arena, she had called on experience and her many gifts to salvage a seemingly lost cause. Master Craftsman was indeed a horse of a different colour; and if the medal itself was not of the metal they might have chosen, it would sit very nicely, thank you, beside that silver horse.

'You vill kiss me!'
The German's gold was a just reward for their great team effort.

'Yahoo!'

CHAPTER NINE

PRIDE COMES AFTER A FALL — AGAIN

One sentence from Britain's individual three-day eventing bronze medallist sums up the immediate aftermath of the Seoul competition. 'There was a *hell* of a party!' For once, the account is inaccurate: Hell was multiplied many times over, for there were parties everywhere you looked. The first was for the Horse Trials Support Group, all the people who had contributed hard cash towards this Olympic effort and had actually got to Seoul to support the team. Rosemary Barlow was the organiser, and there is just a fleeting reference to the fact that Rosemary's face was the unwilling target for a birthday cake baked for one M. Phillips . . .

Ginny has penned, at this stage, a cryptic note in her own diary of events: 'Kiwi party, champagne bottles, wet.' If any gloss on those well-chosen words is needed, it seems to have gone like this: 'The New Zealanders — for whom, of course, Mark Todd had won the individual gold — had invited us to their own party. By the time we got there, everybody was totally out of control.' As luck would have it, there was a water trough — a concrete water trough — on hand. Diners' Club, a part of Citibank, had also turned up trumps with what seemed like a never-ending supply of champagne.

Honest reportage from Ms Leng now resumes. 'If you've got a bunch of people together who have just been through what we all had, and who are basically just a lot of children anyway, there seems, in those circumstances, to be one simple solution to

Team silver and golden smiles plus a big thank-you to Hugh Thomas for a top-flight cross country course.

everything: everybody has to go in the water trough.' The solution was duly applied. 'What we didn't know,' adds our reporter with something of a shiver, 'was that at the bottom of the water trough were a number of bottles of champagne — *broken* bottles. Nobody knew it till the following morning. This thing was only two feet deep, I was just one of those who got dunked — yet none of us was hurt.'

To make matters worse, hard on the heels of the Kiwi party came a function of a slightly more serious nature. 'We had all been invited by the sponsors to go for dinner at the Hyatt hotel, and there just wasn't time to change!' Over to Heather: 'You have never *seen* such a bedraggled lot of specimens. I said to them all, "You *can't* come in like that," but in they duly came. They were all wearing their medals, which

completely threw the security people, for it was early Olympic days and these were the first medals they had seen.' 'They couldn't have cared less supposing we'd had nothing on at all,' laughs her daughter, 'they just wanted to see those medals, so in we went, soaking wet, and we all had dinner.'

Contrary to expectations, after the multiple dunkings and even more numerous celebratory drinks, next morning was, for Ginny, one of the best times in Seoul. 'You wake up and think, "Gosh, it's all over, we've done it," and the feeling was simply wonderful.' There was intense pride as she looked back over exactly what it was she and her teams — Ivyleaze and Great Britain — had done, but there was also time now to savour the rest of the Olympic experience.

'We had just over a week left, during

112

'A quite superb double Olympic Champion with real Charisma — Mark Todd.'

which we were able to relax. This was when Mummy joined the Seoul Club, so the daily diet suddenly improved beyond recognition; and we were able to go and watch some of the other Olympic competi-tion: obviously we supported the show-jumpers and dressage people as much as we could as they got down to their own work, but we also took in some tennis, swimming, hockey . . . Some of the tickets

With Elaine Pickworth — groom extraordinaire.

were readily available, but of course for some of the venues and sports they were in great demand, and like everyone else we had to pay for them. Which meant, of course, getting back in those awful queues . . .'

'Endless official functions' were still the order, it seemed, of every day. As an antidote, the British team decided they should throw their own party for all the other eventing teams, in the indoor school. 'A bit of a bunfight' is the euphemistic description, but here Britain's Olympic silver and bronze medallists came well and truly into their own. On the way back, I. Stark and V. Leng had the bizarre idea of preparing apple pie beds for their unsuspecting friends, the Scot no doubt inspired by memories of the surprise Macbeth had kept in store for *his* own high-born guest. The crime was made all the easier by the fact that Ian had a key for the men's quarters, which were duly invaded and desecrated. It is not true that crime does not pay: it is always handsomely repaid. 'Next morning,' admits Ms Leng, 'into my room stormed a trio of irate show-jumpers. A whole bucket of water went over me and my paper-sheeted bed, and as they stormed out again I pointed out that the least they could do was put on the kettle as they left.' Obliging fellows all (no names, no pack drill), they were happy to grant the request. 'I struggled into the kitchen, feeling not quite one hundred per cent, as can be imagined, made my coffee, took one large gulp — and the little 'bergers' had put neat vodka in that kettle. It tasted like paraffin — I was virtually spitting fire in more ways than one!'

More parties, many hours at the local imitation of Hong Kong's imitation luxury goods store. 'We bought enough Christmas presents for the next few years, I should think. Athletes were actually buying suitcases in which to carry everything they were buying, and there was every kind of athlete you could wish to see.' Not that everyone went financially over the top: the story is also told of a British equestrian competitor, of a Yorkshire persuasion, whose total expenditure during his time in Seoul reached the staggering sum of £2.50 (and the point is in the right place).

Not that the average Olympian has loads of money to spend. 'There was a daily allowance of something like ten dollars, by the Olympic Committee, but the British authorities did not give us any additional money. But of course the contribution had come in actually *getting* us to the Games.' Rumour was rife that certain countries were giving their sportsmen money if they won medals, and some were even said to have been given the equivalent of £60,000 on the spot and a life pension of £8,000 per year. Enough, as Ginny says, to make one change one's nationality . . .

Of course she is not serious, for it was precisely her nationality, and the part she had played in a collective success, that occasioned the greatest pride. 'I think I enjoyed it more than Los Angeles,' she explains, 'because I was what I'd call a grown-up member of the team. Karen was the baby, as it were, and it was rather fun having someone to look after, in that sense, and not be the one that was always being looked after. Having experienced the one before, I knew vaguely what I was doing. I'm not sure it helped in a direct way, but it was good to have been to the Games before because at least you knew what was coming. And we had a lot of fun after the competition was over, going to functions *as a team.*'

Both Ginny and her mother derived much more enjoyment from Seoul than from the previous Olympic venue of Los Angeles. 'The atmosphere was completely different,' says Heather. 'All right, you knew that because of the scale and nature of the Games themselves there was going to be tight security, you would be searched and checked and what have you. But the Koreans themselves were so charming, it was done with such politeness — whereas

I FREELY ADMIT THAT THE BEST OF MY FUN I OWE IT TO HORSE AND HOUND —— Whyte–Melville

SPORTING ART and HUNTING NUMBER

HORSE and HOUND

EVERY THURSDAY 85p (IR £1.24)

September 29 1988

Olympic glory

MARK PHILLIPS' EXCLUSIVE REPORT FROM SEOUL

in the States it had been so belligerent. You knew, too, that you were being done — even while we were there, everything seemed to go up in price, often as much as three times. You knew you were being creamed, all right, but at least it was being done nicely.'

Returning home, the equestrian medallists dutifully took their place in the Heathrow interview queues behind the victorious men's hockey team. Picked up by her agent, Judy Stott, Ginny went straight to a nearby hotel 'for breakfast and a good old yabber' before returning to a village transformed by bunting to receive the local heroine. 'Then we got back here, found a pile of mail a yard high, and it was all rather suddenly back down to earth again!'

Earth, in this instance, was a stretch of Dutch soil known as Boekolo, where Ginny was committed to take part in another international event. 'It was rather too soon for comfort,' she admits, and indeed Boekolo was less than ten days after her return. 'I hadn't been there for ten years or so, and on each previous occasion I'd had a fall. I'd been away off Griffin for many weeks, and I didn't yet know him all that well. Yes, I was a little nervous about taking him to Boekolo. But we went to a cross-country school at Wylye, and he did very well, so that restored some confidence.'

It had been represented to Ginny as a nice CCI cross-country course, that is, one prepared for a Concours Complet International — advanced, but not of Championship level, and a perfect step for Griffin at that stage of his development. 'When I actually walked the course, it was a jolly sight more difficult than I had wanted or expected. But he went well enough to be third, and though I felt I could have ridden him better and he wasn't quite in tune with me, my way of accounting for that is that we didn't know each other very well.'

Perhaps the most enjoyable feature of that Boekolo event was the presence of many of the competitors' families — Mark Todd's wife Caroline, Ian Stark's wife Jennie and their respective children. 'The wives are the ones who do so much of the slogging behind the scenes,' Ginny reminds us, 'and that's a point people often overlook.' The other plus mark for Boekolo, in the aftermath of Seoul, was its abundance of top-class eating places. 'A great treat to be able to walk into a restaurant and get what you wanted when you wanted it! But to be truthful, when I completed Boekolo, I was very relieved. That was the end of the season, and I had simply had enough.'

Ginny's own footnote to the Boekolo trip is the last word on a theme that had run with particular force through this Olympic year: team spirit. 'For me, the most important thing about Boekolo was what one of our sponsors did. Paul Cohen of Citibank drove all the way from England with his wife Pauline and their two children — just to watch me in the show-jumping phase. They couldn't get there for the cross-country, they stayed at the event literally for about four hours, then turned round and drove all the way back home. He felt very strongly about the fact that he hadn't been able to get out to support me in Seoul. Citibank had, in fact, offered Mummy, Dot and me rooms at the Hyatt in Seoul after the competition as a bonus at the end of the Games. I, of course, being such a martyr, declined in order to stay with the team — but I was incredibly envious when I did see the rooms! Then Paul Cohen's gesture in making that long drive to Boekolo was, for me, a very touching end to the year.'

The year had seen Ginny Leng fall from grace off her Badminton horse, pick herself up and pick up a horse of a different kind, endure personal loss and still bounce back to claim unique Olympic fame. She might have felt entitled to a holiday or some other basic human reward, but before she could enjoy the simpler things of life, a further fall awaited her. The Olympic Games had taken her halfway round the world in one direction. When she went the other way, the news was not nearly as good.

'Our sponsors support for us is international.
L. to r., Dot, Uncle Jack, Me, Lady Leng, Ray Malone (President, Diners Club Korea), Mummy, Val Gates, Mr General Manager, Diners Club Korea, and Gerry Rao (Citicorps India). Late for this photocall was my brother Michael and his wife Fiona whose attendance in Seoul cheered me enormously.'

A Press Release

'Eventing is the greatest team sport of them all' — Simon Barnes, *The Times*, 6th May 1988.

'No sex please . . . we're British girls . . . She never competes without her "kinky" boots' — Colin Adamson, the *Evening Standard*, 13th September 1988.

'Three years too long for Lengs' — Nigel Dempster, *Daily Mail*, 2nd June 1988.

These three quotes illustrate some of the principal 'angles' employed by top newspapers in pursuit of their readership ambitions:

— an in-depth look at a sport through one of its top performers, written by a top sports writer
— a headline-grabber to make you turn to the true story written by a 'news' reporter with a sense of humour (!?)
— the sports personality's private life is public property, written by a gossip columnist.

During 1988 and the early part of 1989 Virginia Leng was 'treated' to some overdoses of press interest, a fact which might have left her, and those close to her, particularly Heather Holgate and Dot Willis, somewhat nervous about the roles played by the media in their lives. 'Putting the record straight' was therefore an excellent opportunity for this book.

'Generally speaking the press do a good job for us, and some writers are quite superb' — Ginny.

'It sometimes amazes us that we get so much attention' — Heather, on the sport in general.

'I never quite know whether to say "she's in" or "she's out"' — Dot on Ginny when the press telephone.

All of them are totally agreed about one aspect of their coverage. 'The feature writer that knows nothing about the sport, who never asks the right questions and ignores an agreement to let us see what she has written before it goes to press is the one type of journalist we increasingly don't want to know. They often represent me as a glamorous bird who does nothing all day except ride a few horses, go to parties and look flash in my Porsche.' Ginny's recall of one article in particular evokes strong feelings. 'But the truth is too boring,' adds Heather, motherly and businesslike.

'If I am really busy working horses, attending to sponsors' needs and unavailable, I am often dismissed as snooty. If, at an Event, I am walking the course and really concentrating on my

work, or simply preparing myself for the next stage I really do find it hard to be available to every journalist who wants a quote. We have a perfectly good system for meeting the press at Events so why should I find time to talk to pressmen when *I* should be doing *my* job.' This syndrome, reflected in all other sports is probably the cause of the rash of 'agents' who appear at every turn to 'represent their client's needs'. But in an amateur sport where the cost of a full-time press secretary would be both unviable and inappropriate, the conundrum is exposed.

them such status it is assumed that they can cope. Being a top rider does not mean that you are automatically skilled at handling the media and there have been many occasions when journalists have exploited Ginny's good nature and her 'innocence' with really quite harmful and distressing results.' Ginny accepts that she can be vulnerable and not as hard as some of her contemporaries in other sports. 'I suppose I want the press to like me so that I appear to be a likeable person in print. I think I am a bit naive in some ways.'

There is no doubt that the Team has a list of writers they like and that they will do everything possible to assist them, but despite some of the 'private' pieces written about Ginny during the last year, they are all quite balanced about the 'problems' which do occur with one area excepted. 'No-one likes their private life to be misrepresented and I don't think I'm important enough to attract such attention anyway. But I do get very upset when other people, who are important to me, get dragged in, misquoted or misrepresented and generally made to wonder whether knowing me is worth the trouble.'

On balance then, was the last year fair? 'Yes it was. The equestrian writers did a super job, as did the photographers, the 'news' reporters gave us lots of coverage and most of the feature writers made an effort to understand what I do, even if they did not always reflect this in their article! On a personal level I wish they would stop writing some of the silly, and to me rather childish, things they do such as "golden girl". I am not golden and I am not a girl any more! But all in all they are great.'

Virginia Leng ... ready for a new season after taking a winter break and teaching in the United States

'Publicity for the sport is an important role for those of us at the top,' says Ginny, 'and we can't have it both ways. If we don't help the press we can't expect them to give us coverage. I have got better at it . . . I think . . .' There is a smile. Judy Stott, Ginny's business agent during 1988 has strong views about the subject. 'There is no training scheme for sports stars to learn how to deal with the press. They are not masters of the PR arts and yet because the press gives

'If you had said that Crafty and I
would win any medal at Seoul,
way back at Brigstock in March
'88, I'd have said you were mad.'

CHAPTER TEN:

HORSE IS
A FOUR-LETTER WORD

Scarcely had Virginia Leng shaken the dust of Boekolo from her riding boots than she was adding more miles to an already overloaded year of travel. Her next destination was the United States, partly for personal and family reasons, but also to discharge a duty she had agreed to some time before. Ginny was contracted to conduct a number of 'clinics', or specially-arranged training sessions for up-and-coming riders; little did she know they would lead to a clinic of a very different sort.

The tasks of the teacher had sat less lightly on Ginny's shoulders, when she first undertook them, than she does on a horse. 'My first-ever clinic,' she recalls with something less than joy, 'was in New Zealand in 1981. Because I wasn't very well known at that time, and had very little experience of teaching, it wasn't a big success. I found it very difficult to convince people that what I was trying to teach them wasn't just *my* way of going about things, but one of the right ways. I came in for a lot of criticism — why should they believe me, was the feeling, as at that time especially I was no superstar. The net result was that I lost a lot of confidence in teaching.'

So how had the American trip come about? 'Before I became so busily involved with public relations contracts, I used to do quite a bit of teaching here at the yard in the afternoons, after completing my own work with my horses. I had been asked several years running to go to the States to teach, but kept putting it off and using the

excuse of being very busy — I didn't want to go through that confidence-sapping experience again. I think it was Michael Paige, then chef d'équipe to the American team, who tried again to persuade me — this was in '87. I hadn't given him a final decision when he told me that he'd independently gone and arranged not just one clinic but a series of ten for me to do. I hit the roof, so he came back at me by offering to bring it down to six. So I then felt it had all been virtually done for me, and I'd better give it a go.'

Teaching at six different places in the United States is not quite the same as a quick thrash up and down the English countryside, of course, and there was a great deal of internal flying to do. 'Fortunately for me, I stayed with eventing people wherever I went, people I knew, which made things a lot easier in one sense than they had been all that time ago in New Zealand. It turned out to be a huge success, and I found I really enjoyed the teaching again.' Six clinics, three days each, all over the States, with expenses taken care of by the clinicians — the people in control of the riding schools used as venues. 'It's a very popular idea over there,' Ginny explains, 'much more so than here — because of the sheer scale of the country. Over here, if you really feel like it, you can load up the horse box at any time and go off to see your trainer without facing a thousand-mile trek. In the States they like to go for three days, have a jolly good session and then go back home.'

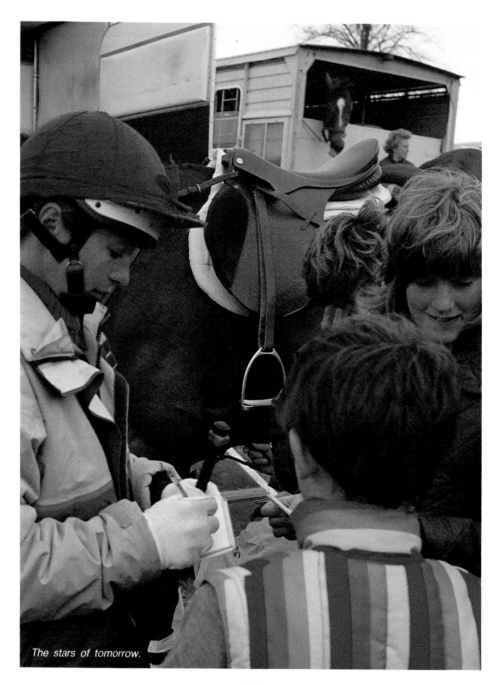
The stars of tomorrow.

124

There would be 24 pupils per clinic, riding every day — dressage, cross-country, show-jumping — and listening to talks and lectures in the evenings, watching equestrian videos and going through an all-round learning process. 'As soon as I finished the last clinic, I flew back to England and was promptly asked if I would do it again the following year. Michael would put everything down on paper for me, dates, locations, travel details, so I just had to wing in, do the job and wing out again without getting bogged down in the administrative side of the whole thing.'

Six clinics in six weeks was a fairly daunting programme, but the enthusiasm from the pupils elicited a similar response from the teacher. 'It's not something I'd want to do every weekend,' she admits, 'but in future I'd be happy to spend some of the time that way — provided I didn't have to organise it all! And on the American front, I don't think Michael Paige will go on holding my hand for ever, but as chef d'équipe he was keen to encourage good cross-country skills.'

The American seminars served a wider purpose, and one dear to this particular lady's heart. They were a forum in which, by discussing her own experience of matters beyond the purely riding skills she could impart, she could stimulate the development of the sport itself. 'I felt that by mentioning PR contracts, sponsorships and so on, I could help encourage other countries to become more involved along those lines. In America, particularly, sponsorship in our sport is non-existent. The sport, over there, is very much in the

The television coverage of Eventing gets better and better.

A nice long rest was Glenburnie's reward for a super 1988.

balance at the moment: to encourage a country of that size to help its individuals and the sport could only have beneficial repercussions for the rest of the world.

'Look at Germany: they, too, were in trouble before the Seoul Olympics, the sport was losing popularity to an alarming degree. Well, having won the gold medal in every possible equestrian arena, everything now is really going strong; they're running five three-day events this year, sponsors are emerging from all sorts of unlikely places, they've been able to go off and buy a couple of horses in North America. So a lot of what I was doing in those evening talks in the States was designed to encourage the riders themselves to go out and find backing. If eventing goes up the creek in America it can only reflect badly on the sport in Europe, too.'

Warming to her subject, this star of the 1984 and 1988 Olympic Games casts her mind forward a further four years. 'As an Olympic discipline, this sport is under strain at the moment. We gather, however, that in 1992 the equestrian side of the Games might be staged in England, not in Barcelona. If it works well, that will be the perfect answer to all those doubting Thomases complaining about the expense of staging equestrian events at the Olympics. If we can make a success of it here, then choose another venue like the United States next time around, the finances won't be a problem and we as a sport will have created something along the same principles as the Winter Olympics — it makes sense, and that's why we are working hard to encourage that way forward.'

One of the ways in which Virginia Leng gives that encouragement is through the time she devotes to her own sponsors. The point, discussed earlier, is worth taking up again as her thoughts turn to Badminton 1989, where on top of her commitment to the competition itself she will spend a great many hours with representatives of Citibank and other personal sponsors. Retain-ing control is the key to her success: 'They have to be well aware of the time span during which I am available — but then if I say I'm going to be with them at four, then I jolly well have to make sure I am.'

Ginny made her retention of control the cornerstone of all her approaches to sponsors. Ground rules were stated, and since then all parties have stuck to them, with few grumbles along the way — and the sport, by its very nature, might have occasioned more. 'There have been occasions, for instance, when I have gone to a major event, something like Gatcombe, where they've gone to a lot of expense on the entertaining front, only for me to turn up and announce I'm not running one of the horses. No problem: I've met with nothing but understanding, when they could legitimately have complained about what I was doing.'

'Always forward', is the Leng motto, and she sees sponsorship — properly understood — as a very positive way forward for herself and her sport. Another would be the creation of more international one-day events, like Gatcombe, with a vital difference. Vets' inspections, till now a feature only of the three-day events, should also be introduced at the one-day variety — before the show-jumping on day three. 'And there should be lots going on,' enthuses the proposer of this idea, 'as at Gatcombe — gun-dogs, celebrities, whatever — to encourage sponsors. A lovely and very different day out for their clients: you haven't got all the Roads, Tracks, and Steeplechase, so you can see everything and get more people on the cross-country course. Therefore there would be an influx of finances, bigger prize money — and so more money into the British Horse Society's coffers with which to encourage their own young riders, set up training schemes to help people get to the top who otherwise might never have had the chance to get there.' The vets' inspection, incidentally, would be Ginny's way of safeguarding the horses from any form of abuse in

The trophies are all remembered.

'The lovely house at Belton Park
— why turn your back on scenes
like this?'

competitions where increased prize money might make the riders try even harder than they already do . . .

America, then, gave Virginia Leng the opportunity not only to renew her enthusiasm for passing on her skills, but also to look to the future of eventing in a wider context. Unfortunately, America also cast a new and threatening cloud over her own equestrian future.

A clinic of a different sort, we said; and it was the final equestrian clinic of Ginny's gruelling tour that did it. It was being held in Oklahoma, where one of the watchers was an orthopaedic surgeon, one Dr Lambert, whom Ginny also met at a subsequent cocktail party. Close friend Mike Huber had observed Ginny hobbling around for a few days. That ankle was clearly still causing her discomfort, and to force her into doing something about it Mike took it upon himself to make an appointment for Ginny with the same Dr Lambert. When they surveyed the X-rays at his clinic in Norman, just outside Oklahoma itself, their worst fears were confirmed.

Not content simply to tackle the Badminton show-jumping arena, the Olympic Games and all the year's other trials on an even footing, Virginia Leng had done so with a fractured left ankle. Insisting that an operation was essential, Dr Lambert himself offered to carry it out. But what if there were complications? The job was delayed only for as long as it took Ginny to get back to England and into hospital, at last to have the problem ironed out.

After the nine months she had just been through, a holiday was very much called for. 'It *has* been a very tough year,' she admitted with characteristic honesty. 'Quite apart from my sporting schedule, trying to sort out my personal life has taken its toll and I feel mentally exhausted. But I feel very positive about everything now, and there is no bitterness.' A major contribution to the restorative process was made by Mike Huber. Not only was he becoming an even closer friend of Ginny's,

his father — also a doctor — had shown increasing concern over her welfare. When the Huber family set off on their planned cruise, it seemed logical that Ginny should accompany them. 'We started from Sydney,' she grins, 'and went to the Bay of Islands in New Zealand, the Fiji Islands, the French Polynesian Islands — it was wonderful, exactly the kind of tonic I most needed. It's perfectly simple: when you're on a boat, nobody can get at you — not even horses! In fact nobody was allowed to mention the creatures: for those few weeks, "horse" was a four-letter word, not a topic of conversation for polite people like us.'

Being on water, however, is like being over the moon: after a while, you have to come back to earth. When Ginny duly docked again, her thoughts turned almost at once to Badminton. 'Make a plan,' is the other Ivyleaze motto, and the plans for 1989 all hinged on her three top horses: Beneficial, Olympic hero Master Craftsman, and the Scottish incomer Griffin.

In one sense, there was no pressure on Virginia Leng this year to go to Badminton come hell or high water, and she did not face the strain of using that event to qualify a horse for future competition. 'But I would like to run Crafty, because I think he deserves to go, and obviously he now has a great deal more experience. I'm also entering Ben and Griffin, and they will be running in at least three advanced one-day events before Badminton itself. It's only during that time that I'll be able to decide which of them will *not* go to Badminton, because of course you are only allowed to compete on two horses. At the moment (March) I must say I'm tending to come down on the negative side, where those two are concerned, for Badminton. Mainly because of the lack of time spent with the horses last season: if I hadn't gone to Seoul I would certainly be running one of them at Badminton.

'But if something happened to Crafty which meant he could not run at Badmin-

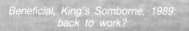
Beneficial, King's Somborne, 1989:
back to work?

ton, I would feel more pushed into taking one of the others despite my misgivings.' The reasons are simple enough, and take up themes which by now should be familiar. 'Because of sponsorship relations, for one thing. They would definitely help sway my mind, given that it's Badminton, and such a special event in its own right.'

By early April, as part of the build-up to Badminton 1989, Ginny had taken all three horses to Weston Park — scene of the clandestine horse trade — and ridden Master Craftsman into fifth place in the Advanced competition. In the Open Intermediate category, Ben and Griffin, though securing modest placings, went well enough to please their rider. Next came an event at King's Sombourne, where Griffin earned his spurs by winning one of the Advanced sections, and Beneficial was second. In another Advanced class, Crafty repeated his earlier fifth place, results which left Ginny well satisfied at that very early stage of a new season.

For once, though, she had regretfully turned down yet another invitation to compete in an unusual one-off competition, a race at Aintree designed to complete a pleasing double alongside the earlier Kempton Park escapade. 'I felt I couldn't really risk Aintree,' Ginny said with no little regret, 'principally because of my leg — why expose myself to further injury after all I've been through with it this year?'

Should anyone doubt the wisdom of that cautious response, Ginny has only to recall a previous painful experience, the breaking of her left arm in no fewer than twenty-three places in 1976. Though the 1988 Badminton fall caused no damage on that scale, she was reminded of it as soon as her recent accident happened. 'Funnily enough, at the time of breaking my arm so badly, it wasn't immediately painful — it just went completely numb with pins and needles. That's how I knew, at Badminton, I must have broken my ankle. I had exactly the same feeling when I tried to stand on it,

it had become completely numb and simply wouldn't accept my weight. That was one more reason why I couldn't believe it when they told me it wasn't broken.' Rehabilitation after the arm injury was agony, so why risk aggravating the later injury?

There were other reasons for not making the Aintree journey. 'I didn't want to pull my retired horses out of their field, either — what a nasty shock that would have been to their very contented systems! And when I weighed it all up, I felt the three chief horses I have here at work now were just that bit too valuable . . .'

Making a plan is a long-term policy too. Given the trials and tribulations of 1988, Ginny Leng was entitled to be taking stock, for one of her most engaging qualities is the ability to view her own career quite dispassionately. 'I've got two more years of sponsorship,' is the frank appraisal, 'and I shall be trying to compete in the European Championships this year, the World Championships next — after all, I have two titles to defend of which I am extremely proud.'

Looking even further ahead, there are more radical choices to be made. 'You have to decide, at some stage, just how much longer you want to continue competing at that level. If you don't, how are you going to move on? Should you go down another road within the sport itself? I feel as if all I've done up until now has been to take from this sport; it's time to be thinking about how to give back, perhaps in an official capacity — a host of decisions have to be made within the next couple of years, not least of all because of the long-term nature of planning my horses' preparation.'

Always concerned to find new and helpful ways of presenting the sport, rather than her own role in it, the notion of becoming a regular television commentator is one that has some appeal. 'There was one point in Seoul where, completely off the cuff, I did a kind of televised walkabout in the Olympic village, and enjoyed it immensely, and I think some of the programmes from and about Seoul did a lot to present our sport in a refreshing and appealing way including Lucinda's expert summaries. For me, though, it would be more interesting — and I could provide useful input, I think — to be on the other side of the camera, offering technical advice that might enhance the viewers' appreciation of all those complex little things that go to make up what we call three-day eventing.'

Always just under the surface, however, is that rich vein of personal pride of performance that determines so much of Ginny Leng's activity. 'The last thing I want to do,' she concludes defiantly, 'is to retire as somebody who *was* good: I want to retire when I *am* good, that's something that's very important to me. If, at the moment, I have no clearly-defined plans, that's also partly because I'm not sure yet how my ankle will stand up to renewed competition. It's not the same as the other, and never will be; it's just a question of how you adapt to it. I managed all right last year, but 1989 is another year again, and who knows? Mind you, I tend to feel that fate takes control of things — it certainly has done in my life, so if I'm not sure about something I tend to sit it out, and wait and see what happens. But as I say, the *last* thing I will do is delay my retirement from top-flight competition until I'm no longer one of the best.'

That cannot be the last word, though, in a story like this. Just around the corner, literally, from Ivyleaze, and just around the corner as Ginny finished the story of her year, was a certain place called Badminton. 'It's a different year, we've got a new course-builder, so it's all just as exciting as it's ever been. There's better prize money, too, which is good for the sport, and what's most important is that the prize money goes further down the line. And it means everybody in the top twelve will get some money to go home with, to help meet the expenses.'

All well and good: but what about another silver horse?

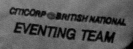
Heather Holgate.

CITICORP BRITISH NATIONAL
EVENTING TEAM